I Got Your
Tailgate
Party
Right Here!

THE BEST OF THE NFL:
NFC EDITION

2

Take one dream, simmer 15 years.
Add the talents of some incredible friends.
Mix well.
Season with the support of family, community, and sponsors, to taste.
Grill at high temperatures for about nine months,
using beer to control any flare-ups!
Remove, let cool, then serve with a smile.
Enjoy, with friends!

Thanks and credit to all who are due... we owe you all a cold one or two!

To Lenny and Nikki, for your friendship and your support. You drove us the whole way, and we'd never have made it without you. Your SPIRIT lives in these pages...
To Bob, for the inspiration, your guidance, and your expertise...
To Rodney and Jill, for your dedication, your patience, and attention to *all* the details...
To Jack Thacker, Jim Charrette, John Deutsch and everyone at Allan Automatic, for giving us the freedom to embark on this adventure and supporting us every mile...
To Roger and Alan at Johnson-Frank for lending us your lot...
To Edward Quinlan and Rick Clemons, for "getting it" and for going beyond the call...
To Lance and Cindi, for making us feel at home when we were so very far away...
To Dan Miller, for giving us our "look" and designing the wrap...
And to Pat, for getting the wrap onto the RV! (And to Angel for letting him help!)
To Travis and Jen, Josh and Tracy, Kat and Brett, Brenda and Rich, Kim and Jeff, for always doing *whatever we ask...*
To Nick, Luc and Frankie, for being with us, always, and through everything...
And to Mom and Dad, for being behind us.
And of course, to the fans and to the friends that we made along the way.

By the grace of God, the love of family, and the power of friendship, we give this gift to you...
Karen and Jay

CONTENTS

Contents

Tricked out Tailgating, 56

Contents

The Tour

It all started with a simple statement. One night, over a hand of poker, Nikki said, rather matter of factly, "You know, my brother Bob always wanted to write a tailgating cookbook."

We were heading down to San Diego for a writer's conference, and said we'd throw the idea out to a few agents and see if there was any interest.

After being told by about a fifty "experts" that we were dreaming, that nobody gets a cookbook published these days unless they are *somebody*, Jay was determined.

They told us, over and over again, "you need to have a *platform*." (That, we learned, is agent-speak for *audience*.)

So we started building one, board by board, nail by bent nail.

We knew from the start this book would be different from other tailgating books, because this book would be about the tailgaters. We would go out to the stadiums--all the stadiums--and meet them on their turf. On the blacktop!

We'd see first hand what they had on their grills, and taste our way across the country in search of the Blacktop's Best. We'd tell their stories and capture on film the complete tailgating experience--the food, the football, and the friends.

We knew we had great plans for our platform, but we still needed a way to pay for the building materials.

Then Jay saw a car driving through our town one day, wrapped in an ad for a fast-food chain. The Tour was born!

The next day, he started making lists and calling companies he thought had products tailgaters could or would use.

After being told by about a hundred marketing and promotions departments that we were crazy, that nobody gets sponsored without hard numbers to back it up, we were discouraged.

"We need to be able to calculate our *ROI*," they'd say. (That, we learned, is marketing-speak for, *cha-ching*.) "Try us again next year after you've got one Tour under your belt."

But Jay kept calling, and eventually, after submitting and resubmitting hundreds of proposals, we were fortunate to find a handful of forward-thinking companies who could see the potential in a grass-roots marketing campaign like ours. They'd get their products into the hands of tailgaters (and campers!) across the country, and we'd be able to write our book!

Camp Chef agreed to outfit our Tour with all our cooking gear, and provide the prizes for our Tailgating Taste-offs. They sent so much stuff, we had to buy a cargo trailer to haul it in!

El Monte RV provided us with a 36' Fleetwood Flair for the season. The day we went to pick it up, Jay spotted it across the lot. YourTailgateParty.com was written on a SOLD tag hanging in the front window. He ran up to it and planted a big kiss right on the grill.

Camping.com said they'd cover our campgrounds every night we were on the road--all 106 of them! They remained in almost daily contact with us, finding RV parks along our route to accommodate us, even after they'd closed for the season in parts of the Midwest!

Our product sponsors, Frank's RedHot, Chaser for Hangovers, 5 Hour Energy, Booyaa, Doyle's Room, Rome Industries, Garpeno, FantasyFootball.com and Bowl-Bound.com kicked in with all the cool samples and give-aways to share with tailgaters and campers, truckers and tollbooth attendants, and anyone else we came across along the way!

Trikke, Freedom Grill, LadderGolf, and PicnicTime gave us their innovative and unique products to demo on the road.

We pledged $50,000 to the Arthritis Foundation, to support research to prevent, control and cure arthritis, the nation's leading cause of disability.

Before we knew it, we were wrapping the Tailgating Tour Coach (in what amounts to an enormous bumper sticker) and loading it up with everything a family of five needs to live--and tail-gate--for four months straight!

The "dream" had become a reality due to the hard work of a handful of "crazy" people we are lucky enough to call friends. Our "Team Blacktop"--Lenny, Nikki, Bob, Rodney, Travis and Pat--had helped us do what everyone said we couldn't do, and we hit the road with our three boys (Nick, Luc, and Frankie) to tailgate at every stadium in the NFC in just one season.

Life on the road was incredible. We drove hundreds of miles nearly every day, homeschooling and working along the way. Days were long, and we were always busy. The kids joked that they never knew when they went to sleep at night which state they would wake up in the next morning. Along the way we visited the greatest cities in America, and fell in love with our country.

The tailgates were amazing. We'd be at the lots, as Nikki said, "before the butt-crack of dawn." In most cases, we had just a few hours to find a spot, set-up, cook, make the rounds of the lot and find contestants, hold the Taste-off, award the prizes, and do our drawings before the game. Nick and Luc would help set-up, then man the give-aways table and videotape the Taste-offs. We could not have done it without them.

We returned home on Christmas Eve, bursting with stories, happy to be back, and ready to begin the real work... writing the cookbook!   -Karen & Jay

The Team...

When you tell people you are writing a cookbook about tailgating, they tend to look at you with a mixture of pity and confusion. I mean, how many ways can you cook a burger, right? So you try to explain about setting up before dawn, about cooking for days, about lobster heads on fence posts and rack of lamb smoking in a custom-built trailer. But until you see it for yourself, until you take a stroll through "the last American neighborhood" it's a little hard to believe.

We started out as a group of friends with a great idea (and without the good sense to wonder why it had never been done before). We set out to write a cookbook that would bring together the best regional recipes from tailgaters across the NFL. What we ended up with is so much more.

We ended up with friends across the country, and these pages are filled with memories of them all. We discovered that beyond the team jerseys and the trash talk, every tailgater is -- at heart -- a football fan.

This is their book.

Kickoff Rub & BBQ Sauce

Team Blacktop's Chef Bob

The secrets behind the ribs that won over LA radio's Mark & Brian at our Kick-off Party...

Ingredients: The Rub

3/4	cup paprika
1	Tbsp granulated garlic
1	Tbsp dried whole basil
1	tsp oregano
1	tsp thyme
1	Tbsp onion powder
1	Tbsp salt
1	tsp white pepper
1	tsp black pepper
1	tsp cayenne pepper

Ingredients:
The Sauce

1 cup ketchup

1 cup chili sauce

1 Tbsp granulated garlic

1 Tbsp onion powder

1 Tbsp Worcestershire sauce

1 Tbsp liquid smoke

2 Tbsp corn syrup

2 Tbsp molasses

1 tsp dry mustard

1 tsp salt

1 tsp black pepper

½ cup apple cider vinegar

½ cup brown sugar

Tasty blends to bring out the best in whatever you've got on the grill...

Mix 'em up and store them in airtight containers, to have on-hand at your next tailgate party!

"Since this is a sandwich that can be eaten with one hand, it leaves the other hand available for your favorite beverage of choice - I recommend an ice cold Labatt Blue!"
     -token Canadian

Beef 'On the Blacktop'

Team Blacktop's Rodney

Ingredients:
The Beef

1	2 lb eye of round roast beef
2	Tbsp shortening
1/4	tsp dry mustard powder
1/4	tsp garlic powder

salt and pepper to taste

12	6" poor boy rolls

Preheat grill to 350 degrees.

Place the roast beef (fat side down) on a wire rack and place that in a disposable aluminum roasting pan.

Spread the shortening on the top of the roast. Sprinkle with mustard, garlic powder, salt and pepper. Cook for 1 hour with the lid closed. Slice for desired thickness.

Ingredients:
The Slaw

1	head of cabbage, shredded	
1	cup	mayonnaise
3	Tbsp parsley, chopped	
1/2	cup	BBQ sauce
1/4	cup	horseradish (prepared)

salt and pepper to taste

(Make ahead, place in resealable plastic storage bag and refrigerate for 24 hours.)

In a large mixing bowl, toss the cabbage, mayonnaise, parsley, BBQ sauce, horseradish, salt and pepper.

Layer the sliced roast beef, on a lightly toasted roll, and top with coleslaw.

13

I Spy...

We've got everything we need to cook anything in the book, right here in our tailgating set-up-- and then some! Can you find...

Cooler *(for food)*
Boiling Pot Set
Keg Roaster
Bean Pot
BBQ Tongs
Frank's RedHot *(in everything!)*
2 Cast Iron Skillets
Big gASS Grill w/ BBQ Box
Heat Guard Gloves
Roasting Forks
Turkey Cannon
BBQ Spatula *(w/ bottle opener!)*
Cooking Thermometer
Scrub Brush
Mixing Spoons
Cutting Board
Portable Gas Fire Ring
Measuring Cup
Ice tub *(for drinks)*
Dutch Oven
Cooking Irons
Single Propane Burner
Table
Apron
Water *(for cooking & cleaning!)*
Aluminum Pot & Basket
Pan Scrapers
Griddle *(triple burner, baby!)*
Mini Dutch Oven
Ultimate Turkey Roaster
Garpeno *(on everything!)*
Can Opener
Chef's Knife
Mixing Bowls
Outdoor Kitchen Tool Set
Towels
Measuring Spoons
Hot Pads
Lighter

The Set-up

Week after week, out on the road and on the blacktop, we put our tailgating set-up to the test. For four months straight, we cooked with this gear every day and were amazed by the versatility of this modular cooking system.

At breakfast it was cinnamon pancakes bubbling on our massive triple griddle. For lunch, pizza pudgy pies toasting over the campfire. And at dinner... whether kebobs or brats or the most amazing steaks from a little butcher shop in Milton, Pennsylvania... we never found a dish (or a crowd!) our gear couldn't handle.

On Thanksgiving, Jay cooked our bird in the Keg Roaster and we baked cornbread in our cast iron skillet.

At a Notre Dame tailgate, Karen made a pot of Navy Bean Soup in our cast iron Dutch oven for the Middies, then baked biscuits with them in the cooking irons over our propane campfire.

Each week, as we walked around the tailgating lots, we'd spot **Camp Chef** gear in action. *Explorer Grills*, the powerful, portable centerpiece of this modular cooking system, with their 60,000 btus of cooking power, seemed to be a popular choice. Since this was the model we were giving away to our winners, we'd always stop and ask how they liked it.

The answer was always the same: "We love it!" Then, these blacktop chefs would tell us about all the great things they'd cooked up. And, they invited us to taste whatever they had on the grill. (Great gig, huh?)

To learn more about our gear, find out where to get it, or check your answers for the I Spy challenge, visit us online at **www.YourTailgateParty.com**.

The Taste-off

These recipes are all winners. Chosen by tailgaters in tailgating lots at every stadium in the NFC, and cooked up by some of the most diehard fans in the entire league. Here's how they ended up in this book...

Every Sunday, we'd pull into the tailgating lots and start looking for the best grub on the grills. We'd walk around, talk with the tailgaters, and invite them to come over for our Tailgating Taste-off. Along with their recipe, they'd bring over a sample of their food for our judges to try.

We recruited our judges out of the lots, too, choosing fans from opposing teams, of all ages, and from all walks of life. The only real restriction is that the judges couldn't be with anyone who was a contestant.

We were always surprised by how seriously these judges took their charge. They would blindly taste each dish (even when it happened to be raccoon!) and carefully consider their choices (usually washing them down with beer in between).

They would take the heckling of the contestants and their supporters with a smile, and confer with each other until a decision was made.

We are grateful to them for their service, and think that they all did a great job.

The first place winners were awarded the title of Blacktop's Best, and took home a brand new Explorer Grill with BBQ Box from Camp Chef. Second and third place winners got other great prizes, and they're in here, too.

Help Choose the NFC Champion Blacktop Chef

Vote for the best recipe in the book. The winning Chef will be competing against the AFC Champion in Canton, OH at the Hall of Fame game in 2007. Make these recipes, choose your favorite and submit this form to: 19713 Yorba Linda Blvd #205, Yorba Linda, CA 92886.

❑Fred Santillan's *Baby Back Ribs*

❑Jason Geer's *Hefeweizen Venison Chili*

❑Paul Thielman's *Hoss' Ribs*

❑Rick Losa's *Stuffed Seahawk*

❑Tim Duffys' *Seahawk Surprise*

❑John Armaly III's *Nightmare Chili*

❑Eric Mitchell's *Zoned Out Surf-n-Turf*

❑Austin Bregman's *Flank Steak*

❑Steve Muck's *BBQ Raccoon*

❑Tim Shanley's *da Bears Bus Beef*

❑Nate Edge's *Falcon 'Souper' Bowl*

❑Bart Beaudry's *Cevapcici*

❑Willie Washington's *Cap'n Willie's Gumbo*

❑Dal Luke's *Bacon Wrapped Venison*

❑Werner Coston's *Kickin' Seafood Gumbo*

❑Lawrence Hughes' *Beer Butt Chicken*

Camp Chef is awarding a Patio Smoker Vault to the winner as well as additional equipment to the runners up. Good luck and Grill on...

Rules and regulations. This original page must be cut out and mailed in. Photocopies or reproductions will not be accepted. Visit www.YourTailgateParty.com for more details.

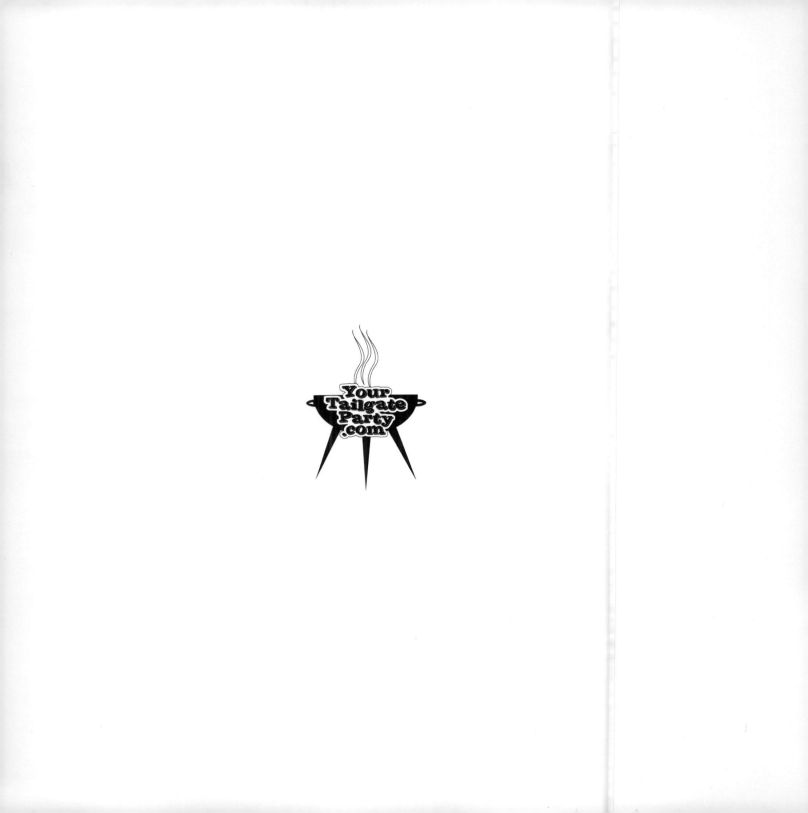

I Got Your
Tailgate
Party
Right Here!

THE BEST OF THE NFL:
NFC EDITION

SAN FRANCISCO 49ERS

Kickin' it at the Stick!

Like it or not, San Francisco has a reputation for putting on some top shelf tailgates. And where we were, in the RV lot, the rep seemed to be well-earned. Our neighbors laid out elaborate buffets of crackers and cheeses and salads, on tables covered with red and gold cloths and sporting fresh flower arrangements. They offered us tastes of their favorite California wines, and were none too impressed when we pulled out our plastic wine glasses!

But that doesn't mean the fans at Monster Park (which they still insist on calling Candlestick) can't throw one MONSTER tailgate! With good weather, plenty of-- CHEAP-- parking, and a great location on the San Francisco Bay, this is a place you'll want to come early and make a day of it. And the 49ers fans do!

All day long, the smell of steaks, lobster tails, and barbecued ribs wafted on the ocean breeze. And after the game, still fired up from their victory (the first win for the first game of the season!) they fired up the grills all over again and partied into the late summer night.

Blacktop's Best...
Baby Backs, Baby!

Blacktop Chef, Fred Santillan

Don't talk to Fred about wine and cheese. This guy spends three days prepping his signature ribs, and parties with some of the most diehard fans on the Bay "near Gate A".

Posing with his dad, fellow 49er fan Fred Sr., this grill master was thrilled to add "Blacktop's Best" to his ever-growing list of awards.

The best thing about *this* recipe? "The majority of time is spent in preparation, well before the tailgate party itself... allowing plenty of time to enjoy the party."

Ingredients:

2	slabs pork baby back ribs - *(about 4 lbs)*

Fred's Dry Rub *(see recipe this page)*

Braising Liquid:

2	cloves garlic, minced
1	medium onion, chopped
2	Tbsp olive oil
2	Tbsp balsamic vinegar
1	cup dry white wine
2	Tbsp white wine vinegar
2	Tbsp Worcestershire sauce
4	Tbsp honey
1/2	cup brown sugar

Prep:

2 Days Before:

Prepare Your Meat!

Wash ribs carefully to remove any bone dust left by the butcher.

Remove any bone fragments from the small end of each rack.

Peel off thin membrane from the inner curved portion of the ribs.

Rinse again and then pat dry.

Cut racks in half or in six to eight inch slabs for ease of handling.

Season the Ribs!

Place ribs on a piece of heavy-duty aluminum foil.

Sprinkle each side generously with the dry rub.

Pat the rub into the meat.

Fold foil around meat creating a sealed packet, with opening at one end.

Loosely fold the opening closed and repeat for all slabs.

Place prepared ribs in the refrigerator overnight.

1 Day Before:

The Secret is the Braising Baby!

Preheat oven to 250 degrees.

Place onion and garlic in medium saucepan on stove. Add olive oil and sweat the mixture until onions are transparent.

Add balsamic vinegar, stir and remove from heat.

Add wine, white wine vinegar, Worcestershire and honey and set aside.

Remove rib packages from refrigerator and open the ends.

Fred's Dry Rub:

Mix equal parts...

Kosher Salt

Paprika

Pepper

Coriander

Dry mustard

Celery seed

Garlic powder

Onion powder

The Ribmaster says...

```
Don't rush the ribs!
Great ribs take
time, but they're
worth every sec-
ond...

Leaving the membrane
in place results in
chewy rib meat,
which won't slide
off the bone...
```

Pour equal amounts of braising liquid into each packet and place on a baking sheet.

Tilt gently, to evenly distribute the braising liquid in each packet.

Braise the ribs in the oven for 2½ hours.

The Killer Secret Sauce

Allow ribs to cool for 20-30 minutes and then pour off braising liquid into a bowl with lid.

Carefully remove ribs from foil packets and place in sealed container.

Place the ribs and the bowl of braising liquid in the refrigerator.

After 1 hour, remove braising liquid from refrigerator and spoon off any congealed fat.

Return liquid to sauce pan, add brown sugar and bring to a simmer.

Reduce until sauce is thick syrup, refrigerate until game time.

Grill:

Game Day

Finish the Ribs!

Place braised ribs on a medium hot grill surface - bone side up.

Grill just long enough to add grill marks and heat ribs thoroughly.

Turn and brush on braising liquid glaze. After one minute, turn and brush more glaze onto bone side.

Turn once more and remove from heat as soon as sauce begins to caramelize.

Serve it up:

Slice each slab into 3 or 4 rib portions, serve and prepare to be worshipped!

Serves 4-6 happy tailgaters. Or just one John Madden!

Grilled Oysters

w/ Chipotle Horseradish BBQ Sauce

Blacktop Chef, Richard Ingram

Ingredients:

4	Tbsp grated horseradish
2	cups tomato sauce
1/2	cup vinegar
1/2	cup honey
4	tsp garlic, minced
2	onions, minced
4	chipotle peppers, minced
2	Tbsp Worcestershire sauce

Soy sauce, to taste

San Francisco sourdough bread

"On a cold foggy day in San Francisco, what better way to get warmed up than eating these hot off the grill oysters with spice. They'll get you going for the game!"
-Richard Ingram

Prep:

Combine all ingredients in a saucepan and simmer for 15-20 minutes. Let cool and keep refrigerated until ready to use.

Grill:

Spoon a tablespoon of BBQ sauce onto each oyster, then place onto medium heat grill. Grill about 5-7 minutes until the sauce begins to bubble and the oysters are cooked through.

Save extra sauce in airtight container in fridge or freezer until next time. This sauce is so tasty, you'll want to try it on everything. Big, juicy steaks just scream for this stuff!

Serve it up:

Serve these babies right out of their shells. They go great with a nice chilled bottle of white wine and some San Francisco sourdough bread.

Shuckin' 101

Oyster, erster. It doesn't matter how you say it, these mollusks can spell tailgating disaster if you don't know what you're doing.

Buy 'em Fresh!

Oysters should be LIVE and tightly closed. No funny smells...

Keep 'em Fresh!

Arrange flat on a tray, cover with a damp towel, and refrigerate for up to one day.

Clean 'em Up!

Scrub shells with a stiff brush in cool water to remove grit.

Open 'em Up!

Use a towel or glove to prevent cuts! Hold oyster firmly; cup-side down, hinge toward you. Slide paring knife between shells at the hinge, and twist to open joint.

Continue sliding knife around edge, keeping it level to reserve liquor.

Scrape inside top shell to detach muscle. Discard upper shell.

Scrape under oyster to detach muscle from bottom shell.

Tailgating in Wine Country!

Fun in any season, and a 49er's game is the perfect reason...

San Francisco is just a stone's throw from Napa Valley, where some of the best wines in the world are produced.

So toss a corkscrew and a cheese slicer in with the ol' tailgating gear, and raise a glass to the best of the Bay Area.

Remember, the key is variety. Offering a wide array of both wines and foods will make it interesting and enjoyable for everyone.

When making your selections, keep these suggestions in mind:

Match flavors. An earthy Pinot Noir goes well with meat dishes, from simple burgers to exotic game and barbecued favorites. The citrus taste of Sauvignon Blanc brings out the flavor of fish (just like squeezing a lemon wedge over a nice piece of grilled halibut...)

Balance sweetness. Beware of serving wine with food that is sweeter than the wine. I like chocolate with Cabernet Sauvignon. I also like chocolate with a good dark beer. Come to think of it, I like chocolate with pretty much anything. Try it with a glass of port, followed by a good cigar... Now that's a party!

Opposites attract? Or in this case, maybe they compliment. Very hot or spicy foods -- think chili or wings -- taste great with sweet wines. Opposing flavors play off each other, creating new taste sensations and cleansing the palate.

Say Cheese! No wine party would be complete without some tasty cheeses, so here's a few hints to help you avoid the Cheez Whiz faux pas!

Red wines go well with mild to sharp cheeses. Pungent, intensely flavored cheese is better with a sweeter wine.

Goat cheeses pair well with dry, white wine, while milder cheeses are best with fruity red wines.

Soft cheese like Camembert and Brie, if not overripe, go with reds like Cabernet, Zinfandel and Burgundy.

-Nikki

"Our group loves to laugh and joke about the Niner fans' reputation of wine and cheese parties before each game.

We laugh hardest while enjoying authentic Santa Maria style grilled tri-tip steaks..."
-Fred Santillan

May we recommend:

Spicy Mozzarella:
    with Zinfandel

Fresh Parmesan:
    with Cabernet Sauvignon

Goat Cheese:
    with Sauvignon Blanc

Aged California Cheddar:
    with Syrah or Syrah Cabernet

Albondigas de Oro

Blacktop Chef, Kathleen Schurter

As unique as the Bay Area itself, this "melting pot" recipe pairs the sweetness of Napa Valley grapes with the spiciness of California's Mexican influences. Surprisingly hot and delicious, this is what the Golden State must taste like!

Ingredients:

1	**large bag frozen meatballs** *(150 meatballs)*
1	**28 oz can red enchilada sauce**
1	**32 oz jar grape jelly**

Prep:

Place frozen meatballs in large pot.

Combine enchilada sauce and grape jelly, then pour over meatballs.

Simmer:

Heat over low flame, stirring occasionally. Beware of getting these too hot, as the sugar from the jelly can burn!

Remove from heat.

Serve it up:

Serve meatballs from the pot to keep them warm. Provide toothpicks for poking.

Serves 30 people (5 meatballs each), but be sure to get yours quick or they'll be gone!

"These yummy meatballs are always the first to disappear at a tailgate! They're easy, no one can guess what's in them, and they go great with beer!"
-Kathleen Schurter

San Francisco 49ers

Team Blacktop Tip:

Our large cast iron Dutch oven worked great for this recipe. It kept the meatballs good and warm long after we removed it from the grill. (And it looked cool, too!) Get yours from our Tour Sponsor Camp Chef at www.CampChef.com!

SEATTLE SEAHAWKS

Tailgating in "Heaven"

Hardcore Hawks fans call this place heaven. A quarter-mile strip of parking lot, sandwiched between the Viaduct and a row of shipping warehouses just west of the stadium, it's home base for several of Seattle's most loyal tailgating groups.

They show up early and stay all day, starting off with plenty of coffee (locally roasted, of course) before moving on to the beer (locally brewed).

On the grill you'll find a variety of seafood (all locally caught) as well as game like venison and elk (locally shot). You getting the picture?

These folks live, eat, and drink the Northwest, and their Seahawks are no exception. So you can imagine what a season it was when their team rode that wave of local pride all the way to SuperBowl XL!

And with the same brand of optimism that could build an open-air stadium in a city renowned for its rainfall, any Hawks fan will tell you to watch out for a win... next season.

Blacktop's Best...
Hefeweizen Venison Chili

**Blacktop Chef,
Jason "Uncle J" Geer**

We first met Uncle J at a Monday night game during the '04 season, and our mouths were watering just knowing we'd get another chance to sample his legendary dish.

"This chili is the BEST! I have to keep making more and more every time, and still I never come home with any leftovers! It has made our tailgate grow in numbers because everyone wants to taste my chili."

Ingredients:

12	lbs meat, cubed or ground -

Venison has the best flavor, but you can substitute beef, chicken or pork...

1	large yellow onion, chopped
1	large white onion, chopped
2	4.5 oz jars minced garlic
16	Hefeweizen beers, room temp
10	1 oz packs chili seasoning
3	24 oz cans tomato sauce
2	16 oz cans Mexican-style stewed tomatoes
2	16 oz cans black beans
2	16 oz cans chili beans
2	16 oz cans kidney beans
2	24 oz cans pickled whole jalapenos
10	fresh habanero peppers
1	2 1/2 oz jar chili powder
	hot sauce

```
"I use 5 different brands of
hot sauce because I like it
hot!  You can use less or
more depending on your taste.
Come on, don't be afraid. Pour
the whole jar in!"
                        -Uncle J
```

Prep:

1 Day Before:

Drain all liquid out of cans – the only liquid added is beer!

Put 4 beers in 25 quart stock pot and add meat, 1 jar garlic, chopped onions, and some hot sauce.

Brown meat, do not drain yet. After the meat is cooked, add the rest of the ingredients (leaving beer for last).

Fill almost to the top with beer, mix well and bring to a simmer. Simmer for at least 12 hours, stirring every hour and spooning off excess grease as it accumulates.

Refrigerate overnight.

Simmer:

Game Day:

Arrive early, and start chili simmering on a portable gas burner. As a hungry crowd starts to gather around the amazing aroma, slowly bring the chili up to a boil.

Serve it up:

Carefully spoon into bowls (or you can use bread bowls), and top off with cheese, crackers, and chopped onion. This recipe will easily feed more than fifty tailgaters!

Pasta Tinoisamoa

Blacktop Chef, Scott Johnson

Try this tailgating tradition with a tasty Hawaiian twist...

Ingredients:

1	lb bow tie pasta
1	lb wheel pasta
1	red bell pepper, diced
1	green bell pepper, diced
1	pack of Feta cheese
2	heads broccoli, chopped
1	bottle Italian dressing

EZ Prep:

Cook pasta, rinse and cool. Cut vegetables and mix all together with dressing. Chill and serve.

The Twist:

Substitute broccoli with diced pepperoni, olives, pineapple (why not, you love it on pizza!) and SPAM (yep, Hawaiians dig it!) Da kine!

Local Flavor

What do a "Sausage King," a brothel and Seahawks fans have in common?

Mikey, and the Triangle Pub!

This Seattle fixture fills a triangle kitty-corner from the Seahawk's stadium. Its historic significance as a brothel, and the fact that Mikey "the Sausage King" grills fresh sausages right out on the sidewalk, makes this a great place to stop by for a beer and a bite before the game, or anytime for that matter!

On Mikey's invite, we stepped up for a sample, then were lured inside by the beer and cheer. Wandering through the Triangle and enjoying the taste of fresh linked sausage and local microbrews, the game day "regulars" welcomed us warmly into what they insisted is the "best damn bar in Seattle!"

-Jay

Kalbi Steak

Blacktop Chef, Dave Black

This simple dish, a nod to the Asian influences upon Seattle cuisine, is easy to prepare and share with the whole group. You can grill it in steaks, like Dave did, or skewer the meat up into some mouth-watering kebabs.

And once you've become addicted to this sauce (and we know you will!) Dave suggests you try it on chicken or pork, the traditional Korean short ribs, or even fresh grilled veggies!

Ingredients:

4	lbs flank steak

Kalbi Sauce:

2/3	cup soy sauce
3	Tbsp water
3	Tbsp honey
3	Tbsp sugar
1	Tbsp sesame seeds, roasted and ground
2	Tbsp sesame seed oil
2	cloves garlic, crushed
2	Tbsp green onions, chopped
1-2	bags mixed salad greens

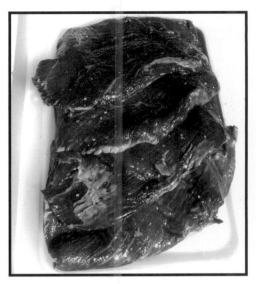

Prep:

Mix all sauce ingredients in bowl using whisk until blended thoroughly. Pour into gallon-sized zipper bag. Place flank steak into bag and close tight.

Shake bag, carefully, to cover meat with sauce.

Refrigerate overnight.

Grill:

Grill over medium-high heat until barely pink inside.

Serve it up:

Slice into strips and lay on bed of mixed salad greens. This may be one of the healthiest dishes you'll ever find at a tailgate, but we guarantee it's also one of the tastiest!

Cedar Plank Salmon

Blacktop Chef, Kim Harris

Salmon has been both the lifeblood and the soul of the Pacific Northwest for as long as humans have been fishing its' rivers. Whether smoked, grilled, poached or blackened, the preparation of this pink, flavorful meat is almost a sacrament in Seattle, and here's a classic recipe that is sure to do it honor.

Try this!

-Cut your salmon fillet and your plank into individual-sized pieces and serve it up right on the plank!

-Experiment with different types of wood, like mesquite, cherry, oak, apple, and alder for different tastes.

Ingredients:

1	3-5 lb salmon fillet
1	stick of butter, melted
2-3	fresh lemons, sliced 1/4" rounds
2-3	Walla Walla sweet onions, sliced
1/2	bunch fresh dill, chopped
1/2	bunch fresh dill, whole
	sea salt and coarse ground pepper
6x12"	cedar plank *(from your local BBQ or hardware store)*

Prep:

Soak the cedar plank in water for 2 hours. Preheat grill to med-high. Rinse salmon under cold water and pat dry.

Place salmon in the center of the cedar plank, skin side down. Drizzle half the butter over the salmon. Sprinkle fresh chopped dill over the entire fillet.

Arrange lemon slices and onion slices, overlapping, down the center of the salmon. Place 1 or 2 larger sprigs of dill on top of the lemons for presentation purposes.

Grill:

Grill until light pink and flaky.

Pike Place's Flying Fishmongers!

Fresh Fish!

Choose your salmon wisely. A good piece of fish will make you a hero, and a bad piece will net you a bucket full of chum.

Buy your salmon from a market that keeps it very cold. Laid out on a clean bed of ice in a refrigerated case is the best.

A fresh catch should smell like the ocean. A bad smell is the sign of an old or inadequately chilled fish.

Always check to see if the flesh will bounce back after you press it with your finger. If it doesn't, keep looking.

Now, look deep into the eyes. Are they cloudy or sunken? If so, stay back!

Also, make sure that the fish is clean and pink.

Don't hesitate to go to another market if you find bad fish.

Once you take it home, keep it in the coldest part of your fridge or ice chest until you're ready to cook it.

-Jay

Seattle Seahawks

Not only do they produce some tasty beers, but local brewpubs can be a fun place to visit on gameday -- or any day! They often offer tours of the brewery, taster trays that allow you to sample a wide selection of beers, and menus that showcase their brews in sauces, marinades, and -- one of our favorites -- spent grain breads!

Downtown Seattle has more than a few to choose from, some in the immediate vicinity of the stadium.

Check out:

Elliott Bay Brewing Co.

Elysian Brewing Company

Gordon Biersch Brewing Co.

Hales Ales

Pyramid Alehouse

The Pike Pub and Brewery

It's all about the beer!

The heart of any Seattle tailgate (or any Seattle party, picnic, or Saturday afternoon for that matter) is a great bottle of beer from one of the Northwest's famous microbreweries. So to help you pick the perfect variety to pack into your cooler for gameday, we've come up with a list of a few of our favorites…

Hefeweizen is an unfiltered wheat beer with a smooth, crisp flavor. Serving this beer with a lemon wedge has become a Northwest tradition! Serve it with salmon and you'll look like a local!

Light only by name, this is no stupid beer! Blonde Bock Lager is a malty beer with a tint of bitterness and slight aroma — it's great with appetizers or a sandwich and salad.

A nutty, toasted chocolate flavor is what you'll find in your typical Brown Ale. Enjoy this with brats, or baby back ribs.

"Beauty is in the hands of the beerholder."

If you've got steaks or burgers on the grill, you might want to go more toward a Stout. I love Stout, but it fills me up too fast. So try a Porter. It will give you the smooth, rich taste that a Stout would, and still leave room for another!

Not a big beer fan? *(ssshhhh! Don't say that too loud!)* Most microbreweries have Hard Cider offerings that are a great alternative to coolers or malt beverages. For something crisp, look for a Pear. A little heartier, go for the Apple. Or if you want to really impress your friends, mix half Brown Ale and half Raspberry Cider!

-Jay

Now You're Cookin'

Beer seems to be, inarguably, the tailgater's drink of choice. But, the true blacktop chef is one who "thinks outside the bottle" and knows the true versatility of a good brew.

Make your meat "merry"! Soak your favorite meat in a beer bath to add flavor and tenderize at the same time.

Excellent choices for beef include Porters and Bocks. Avoid anything too hoppy, as they tend to dry out your meat. Throw in some garlic, onion, and Worcestershire for a classic taste.

For chicken, go with a Pale Ale. Something with nice citrus tones works well. Or, we love to soak our birds in Corona, with lime, garlic, and cilantro.

Spice up your seafood with a full-bodied Amber and a dash of Cajun seasoning. It's great for shrimp!

Soup up your stews! One for the pot, one for the cook. That's the rule around our grill! Why add water when you can add FLAVOR to your favorite stew, soup and chili recipes? Beer adds depth and complexity to the dish (kinda the opposite of what it does to the chef!)

Perk up your pancakes! It may sound strange, but Team Blacktop's Lenny throws a little beer into his griddlecakes. He swears that the flapjacks are fluffier because of the bubbles. He likes a light beer, but have some guts. Try adding the heartiness of an Oatmeal Stout or chocolate notes of a nice dark Porter.

Boil your Brats! *Before* throwing them on the grill, let your bratwurst sweat it out awhile in a pot of boiling beer. See page 66 for a great recipe!

Quench the fire! Always be sure to have a beer in hand when grilling fatty meats (like you didn't do that anyway!) When the dripping fat starts a flare up, douse the flames with a splash or two. It prevents burning while adding a nice, caramelized glaze to your meat.

Yes, you can! Beer can chickens are all the rage, and most people know that this method of steaming a chicken from the inside over a can of your favorite beer produces a moist, flavorful bird, unrivalled on the grill. Try our winning recipe on pages 96-97!

Simmer down! Reduce beer by half in a saucepan, then combine with ketchup, brown sugar, garlic, liquid smoke, etc. for a tasty homemade BBQ sauce.

And at the end of the day, when the cooking's done and the raves are rolling in, crack open another because the best part is... you can drink it, too!

MINNESOTA VIKINGS

Skol Viks!

Having an enormous stadium in the heart of a city is cool. There's an energy, an excitement, that bounces building to building as fans fill the crowded streets and break out the barbecues to party in every nook and cranny, driveway and alley.

Parking, however, can be hard to find in downtown areas. And expensive! In fact, Minneapolis had the most expensive tailgating we found for an RV. Private lots near the stadium were charging up to $400 per vehicle!

The Vikings encourage fans to tailgate at Rapid Park, a commercial lot about a mile and a half northwest of the stadium. They offer reasonable rates, plus all the amenities tailgaters come to appreciate, like portable toilets and garbage cans. As added incentive, fans are treated to live music, appearances by the Vikings' cheerleaders, and free shuttle service to the Metrodome before and after the game.

But many hardcore fans prefer to party within view of the stadium, so they pack the lots just north of the stadium off Washington. And that's where we found our Blacktop's Best...

Blacktop's Best...
Hoss' Ribs

Blacktop Chef, Paul "Hoss" Thielman

We met Hoss when he was feeding a ton of people from his enormous grill full of ribs. Hoss is the Executive Chef at *The Mink's Nest*, a delivery truck built out with a bar/lounge. The whole thing is painted purple, with the Vikings logo and jerseys with the names of Hoss and his buddies. And behind it, a complete kitchen trailer with everything an extreme tailgater needs to feed the big crowd that's sure to gather around a killer set-up like this!

Ingredients:

4	racks of spare ribs
2	cups soy sauce
2	cups teriyaki sauce
1	cup onion, chopped
1	clove garlic, chopped
1	cup balsamic vinegar
1/2	cup Italian dressing
1/4	cup steak sauce
1/4	cup mustard
2	Tbsp of Worcestershire sauce
2	Tbsp salt
2	Tbsp course ground pepper
2	Tbsp Lawry's Seasoned Salt
2	Tbsp lemon pepper
2	Tbsp cocktail sauce
1/4	cup of honey

Prep:

Mix all of this in a resealable container that is large enough to cover the ribs completely. Place the ribs in the marinade and cover in the refrigerator for at least 12 hours. You can cut your ribs into serving size portions before they go in the marinade.

Grill:

Slow cook the ribs on low heat for about 1 1/2 hours. Keep a container of liquid on the grill to keep the ribs moist.

Extra point:

This marinade can be used with just about any cut of meat, from chicken to ribs to tri-tips. Enjoy!

Breakfast Cookies

Blacktop Chef, Roxy Soll

"These are great for early AM tailgating. They have all the best ingredients for a healthy breakfast… oatmeal, Wheaties and peanuts for protein! These are made ahead of time, and that means there's more time at the party for drinking, passing around the football and other fun stuff."

Ingredients:

1	cup butter
1	cup sugar
1	cup packed brown sugar
1	tsp vanilla
2	eggs
2	cups oatmeal
1	cup Wheaties or Cornflakes
1	tsp baking soda
1/2	tsp salt
1	cup peanuts

EZ Prep:

Preheat oven to 350. Cream together butter and sugars. Add 2 beaten eggs and vanilla, mix well. Add all remaining ingredients and mix well. Drop by teaspoonfuls on cookie sheet; flatten with glass dipped in sugar. Bake at 350 for 12 minutes.

Tailgating Rules!

Know 'em & Live 'em!

ALWAYS abide by the 4-Hour rule:
Be set up a minimum of 4 hours before game time!

Grills are REQUIRED:
It's not really a tailgate unless something gets cooked on the spot!

No NAGGING Wives, Spouses or Significant Others!

Hometown Consumption:
Always drink beer that is brewed in your home state!

What happens at the Tailgate stays at the Tailgate!

Beer Exchange Rule:
When you are on the road, always offer an exchange: One of your local beers for one from a local tailgater!

Don't Give the Police a Reason to Arrest You—
Before or After Game Time!

Courtesy of Mookie. For the whole story, visit www.vikingstailgate.com.

BBQ Brisket

Blacktop Chef, Scott Theis

Scott, and his wife Kim, had made an awesome brisket, along with some New Orleans' style gumbo that Scott literally threw together without a recipe – Good stuff! They cook this brisket because it's easy and it's a tailgating staple!

Scott's group had a ton of cool tailgating paraphernalia that were all painted up in Viking colors including a keg grill and homemade drink stand.

Ingredients:

1	6-8 lb beef brisket
1	18 oz bottle ketchup
½	cup brown sugar
½	cup water or red wine
¼	cup Worcestershire sauce
2	packages onion dried soup mix

Hamburger buns

Prep:

Mix ketchup, brown sugar, soup packets, water, wine, and Worcestershire sauce.

Place half of the mix on the bottom of a cast iron Dutch oven. Place the brisket in the Dutch oven and pour the remaining mix over the top of the brisket.

Simmer:

Slow cook for 6-8 hours in a cast iron Dutch oven over a low flame.

Serve it up:

When the meat shreds easily, cut it across the grain and serve it on a bun.

Team Blacktop Tip:

Try with an onion or cheese kaiser roll.

Pudgy Pies

Blacktop Chef, Joni Tikalski

These camping classics translate perfectly into the tailgating lot. "Pudgy Pies are a party on a stick!"

Equipment:

Cooking Iron, Cooking Spray and an Open Flame.

How to:

Spray your iron with cooking spray. Place a thin tab of butter in both sides. Make a sandwich out of your bread and filling. Put the sandwich in the iron and close the iron. Place the iron on the fire. Cook until the bread is toasted to your liking. Open the iron and dump your pie on a plate. Let it cool before you bite!

Breakfast:

1	can favorite fruit pie filling
1	gallon resealable bag
1	cup powdered sugar
1	stick of butter
1	loaf of bread

Shake the pie in the powdered sugar and eat! Careful, these babies can be hot!

Lunch:

Favorite lunch meat

Favorite cheese

Mustard, mayo, ranch dressing, etc.

1	stick of butter
1	loaf of bread

Dessert:

Chocolate chips, marshmallows, peanut butter, Nutella, etc.

1	stick of butter
1	loaf of bread

Combine some or all of your favorite sweets. Be creative!

Superfans!

They have names like Arrowman, Bone Lady, Ramman and Big Nasty. They wear colorful costumes, and sport outrageous hairstyles. Their sometimes-frightening rituals often involve burning and impaling.

They're a tribe whose members know no borders; social, economic, or geographic. They are the Superfans… and they DON'T wear MAKEUP!

"It's FACE PAINT," insisted Vikings fanatic John Velek as he handed us his trading card featuring a photo of him all decked out as his alter ego, Super V-Man. And who's gonna argue with a guy wearing a horned Viking helmet?

He and his buddy, fellow Superfan Patrick "The Spiking Viking" Olsen, are inductees into the Pro Football Hall of Fame's Hall of Fans. Like all the Superfans we met out on the blacktop, they spend hours getting ready for the pre-game activities, and are always more than happy to stop and strike a fearsome pose for the camera.

35

WASHINGTON REDSKINS

Who doesn't love a 'Skins game?

It's hard not to cheer for the Redskins, even when they are playing your team.

We found that out when we showed up to watch the battle of Washington vs. Washington, East vs. West...

I mean, there you are in the nation's capital, surrounded by history and monuments and power... and then there are the Redskins, AMERICA'S home team, with a rich history of their own and a record not easily dismissed. It's almost a matter of national pride. It feels unpatriotic to be against them.

Until they try to serve you your team's mascot, stuffed with ham and sticky with a delectable glaze. The SAVAGES!

Here we met some of the most fun-loving, diverse, and devoted fans around, and they really knew how to put out the welcome mat!

Fed-Ex Field is a great place to tailgate, with plenty of parking at the stadium, and an active tailgating community.

Blacktop's Best...
Stuffed Seahawk

Blacktop Chef, Rick Losa

"We've been at every home game for the Washington Redskins for the last 15 years. Friends, family and sometimes even celebrities stop by because we are legends!

We've even had the Cowboy Cheerleaders come by the bus to party with us."

He's right, everyone told us to go see Rick! And were we glad we did! A big Hawaiian guy who loves cooking big, Rick and his 12th Man Crew inaugurated us into the D.C. world... of tailgating. Thanks!

Ingredients:

boneless chicken breast

honey-glazed ham, thick sliced

1	packet Caribbean jerk seasoning
1/4	cup garlic, chopped
1/2	cup onions, diced
1/2	cup mushrooms, sliced

salt and pepper to taste

1	Tbsp olive oil

Prep:

In a small bowl, combine jerk seasoning with oil and a little bit of water to make a spice paste. Add chopped garlic, diced onions, salt, pepper and sliced mushrooms.

Butterfly a boneless chicken breast, open it up and add a good slice of the honey-glazed ham. Spread the mixture over the chicken and wrap in foil.

Grill:

Slow cook on med heat until chicken is cooked through and life is good!

Serve it up:

Slice the chicken like thick bread, use a toothpick to keep it together, serve with rice pilaf and teriyaki broccoli. Enjoy!

Grill the Opponent...

Around the tailgating lot, stories abound of tailgaters going to extremes. There are the Green Bay fans who, legend has it, traditionally cook bear whenever they're playing Chicago.

So, we looked a bit suspiciously at Rick Losa when he told us "Stuffed Seahawk" was on the menu for the day. "Imported, fresh from Seattle," he insisted.

We were more than relieved to find on the grill his variation of chicken cordon bleu.

When it comes to keeping with the tradition of cooking your opponent, tailgaters can get pretty creative. We tasted "Falcon & Dumplins" and "Dead Falcon Parmesan" in Carolina, "Seahawk Surprise" and "Buffaloed Seahawk Dip" in St. Louis.

If you're playing the Saints, seems anything Cajun will do. Facing the Rams? Better cook lamb. The Dolphins often inspire seafood on the grill, and Green Bay's a great excuse to whip up something cheesy.

Southern Maryland Pulled Pork

Blacktop Chef, Mike Zdobysz

Mike loves to cook for big crowds, and any tailgate will do just fine!

Team Blacktop Tip:

Cooking with wood chips adds flavor to the food and bodies to the tailgate. You can buy cherry, mesquite or hickory chips in most stores. Always soak your chips in water for at least 2 hours. I like adding flavor to my chips by adding Jack Daniel's and salt and pepper to the water. I spread the chips evenly in a foil pouch with holes poked in the top and put it right over the open flame.

-Jay

Ingredients:

1	4 lb pork roast
1	Tbsp Worcestershire sauce
1	Tbsp salt
1	Tbsp pepper
1	Tbsp liquid smoke
2	shakes Old Bay Seasoning
2	shakes hot sauce
2	shakes hot pepper flakes

Mike's Mom's Sauce
(recipe follows)

Soaked wood chips

Prep:

Combine ingredients and mix well. Pour sauce over the pork in disposable aluminum pan. Put on grill with soaked wood chips.

Grill:

Slow cook on low heat 4 hours or until pork is done. Pull pork off bone and shred. Let cool, then pour sauce over it and simmer.

Serve it up:

Get some rolls and chow down.

Mike's Mom's Sauce

Ingredients:

6	Tbsp olive oil
3	Tbsp Worcestershire sauce
2	Tbsp apple cider vinegar
3/4	cup ketchup
1	clove garlic, chopped

Prep:

Combine the ingredients and simmer for 45 minutes in a sauce pan, stirring occasionally.

Chris Irwin's Redskin Ribs

Blacktop Chef, Chris Irwin

Ingredients:

Pork ribs

Irwin's *Secret* Rub

Irwin's *not-so-secret* Sauce:

1/2	cup ketchup
1/4	tsp brown sugar
1	tsp basil

Garlic salt to taste

Salt and pepper to taste

Prep:

Cover ribs with salted water and bring to a boil for 20 minutes. Remove from water and cool. Rub cooled ribs with Irwin's secret rub.

If you don't have clearance, substitute Kickoff Rub (page 12)!

Grill:

Slow cook for 2 hours on low heat turning occasionally.

Serve it up:

Toss cooked ribs in sauce and serve.

'Big Grin' Beans

Blacktop Chef, Pat Murphy

Ingredients:

1   lb bacon, diced
(Farmer John, thick-sliced)

2   lbs sausage, quartered
(turkey and/or pork kielbasa)

1   large white onion, diced

1   large can each:

　　Bush's Baked Beans,
　　Bold & Spicy

　　Van Camps Baked Beans,
　　Honey & Ham

2   cans butter beans, drained
(I use approx. 1 & 3/4 cans)

1/2 cup brown sugar

1/2 cup ketchup

1/2 cup BBQ sauce

EZ Prep:

Fry the bacon until crispy.

Brown kielbasa in a cast iron Dutch oven.

Mix BBQ sauce, ketchup, brown sugar and onion in separate bowl.

Put all the ingredients into a cast iron Dutch oven and slow cook for 3 hours.

39

ST. LOUIS RAMS

Meat Me in St. Louis

Somehow, while grilling up ribs and tossing around a football before a Rams home game, you just can't shake the knowledge that you're tailgating on the Mississippi!

Most of the lots are located along 3rd Street between the stadium and the river bank, and you can almost feel the pulse of America flowing up this central artery.

Here, in the shadow of the famed St. Louis Arch, the Old Muddy flavors the day in the spices and seafood it carries upriver from New Orleans, and the sounds of the Blues that hang in the air.

Nearby, Laclede's Landing brings together a taste of old St. Louis with a fun collection of shops, pubs, and entertainment.

Though the Rams are relative newcomers to this historic city, they've built up a loyal fan base in their new hometown, and can boast some of the best tailgating in the NFL!

Blacktop's Best...
Seahawk Surprise

Blacktop Chef, Tim Duffy

Tim and his "mob" of tailgaters pulled into the lot with trailer in tow. Their set up had all the comforts of home, including TV, stereo and even a couch! When we invited them over to the Tailgating Taste-Off, Tim got creative. He made up this recipe on the spot with items he had to gather from nearby tailgaters. "In keeping with the time-honored tradition of eating your opponent, "Seahawk Surprise" combines seafood and fowl with juicy pork tenderloin that will make you ask for more."

Ingredients:

1   2 lb pork tenderloin

1   lb shrimp

1   dozen chicken wings

Bag shredded "four cheese blend"

Salt and pepper

Grill:

Grill the chicken and shrimp, set aside. Season tenderloin with salt and pepper and grill at medium-high heat for about 25-35 minutes or until done.

Prep:

While the tenderloin is cooking, peel shrimp and remove chicken meat from bones. Dice the shrimp and chicken and mix together. Slice open tenderloin and hollow out to make room for the surprise. Stuff with mixture and cover with cheese. Place it on the grill just long enough to melt the cheese.

Serve it up:

Slice and serve.

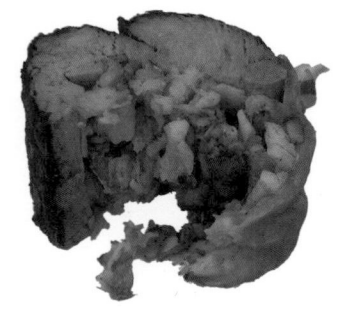

Stuffed Portobellos

Blacktop Chef, Jeff Weiss

Ingredients:

12   portobello mushrooms

1/4   cup balsamic vinegar

3/4   cup olive oil

2   Tbsp garlic, minced

2   tsp dried oregano

Cracked black pepper to taste

2   jars marinated artichoke hearts, drained and chopped

4   oz crumbled bleu cheese

Prep, Grill, and Serve:

Rinse and dry mushrooms. Marinate in vinegar, olive oil, garlic, oregano and pepper for at least 2 hours. Remove mushrooms from marinade, then remove and chop stems. Mix stems with bleu cheese and artichoke hearts. Stuff the mushroom caps with mixture. Grill on high heat until cheese is melted and mushrooms are heated through. Slice and serve with toothpicks on a platter.

Al's Famous Bloody Mary Blend!

Blacktop Chef, Alan Lueff

We tasted Bloody Marys across the country, and we have to tell ya, Al's are some of the best!

Ingredients:

1   bottle SKYY Vodka

Jalapeno-stuffed olives

Celery stalks

Ice

Mary Mix:

2   64 oz bottles Hot & Spicy V-8 juice

1   Tbsp celery seed

1   Tbsp celery salt

1/2   cup Worcestershire

2   Tbsp fresh, ground horseradish

1/2   cup fresh squeezed lime juice

Cracked pepper

EZ Prep:

Pour vodka and Mary Mix together over ice in cup and garnish with celery stalk and olive.

Rick's Rub

Ingredients:

1/4 cup paprika

3 Tbsp brown sugar

1 tsp garlic salt

3 tsp garlic powder

3 Tbsp onions, minced

3 tsp black pepper

Kosher salt to taste

Prep:

Combine ingredients and mix well.

We ran into tons of cool tailgating toys at every stadium. We saw BBQ trailers, flat screen TVs, Six-Bottle liquor wheels, inflatable goal posts, and the coolest beer coozies around!

42

Hog Wild Pulled Piglet

Blacktop Chef, Rick Caminiti

Ingredients:

2-3 bottles dark beer

2 Tbsp minced garlic

1 6-8 lb pork butt

Rick's Rub

Prep:

Rub Rick's Rub on pork.

Grill:

Smoke in smoker (with charcoal or hickory wood) for 6-7 hours.

Put in cast iron Dutch oven for 4-5 hours until easy to shred. Pour dark beer in Dutch oven while cooking.

After pork is shredded, add minced garlic and stir. Simmer in Dutch oven on grill for 1 hour.

Serve it up:

Serve on a kaiser roll or your favorite bread roll, or try Mere's Rolls.

Mere's Rolls

Blacktop Chef, Pauline Richard

These rolls are SO good. Mere said she's been making these babies for more than 60 years, and it takes practice to get them just right. Of course, hers always come out perfect!

Ingredients:

2 packages dry yeast

3 tsp sugar

1/4 cup margarine

1 cup milk

2 eggs

1 tsp salt

9 cups flour

Prep:

Mix 1/2 cup lukewarm water (Mere calls it "baby bottle" warm), the yeast and sugar. Let stand for 10 minutes.

Add the melted margarine, 2-1/2 cups water, warm milk (105-115 degrees), eggs, salt and 2 cups of flour. Mix together and let stand for 1 hour.

Add remaining flour and knead for 10 to 12 minutes. Let stand for 2-1/2 hours

Shape into rolls and place in a slightly greased baking pan. Let stand in pan for 1 hour.

Cook:

Preheat oven to 350 and bake for 20 minutes or until golden brown.

Serve:

These rolls are perfect for Rick's Pulled Piglet and add a great touch to any meal.

Buffaloed Seahawk Dip

Blacktop Chef, Sue Crean

According to Sue, this dip is requested everywhere she goes. We had a taste, and this dip will knock your socks off.

Ingredients:

3	lbs chicken breast, grilled & shredded
12	oz cream cheese
12	oz shredded cheddar cheese
8	oz ranch dressing
8	oz Frank's RedHot Buffalo Wing sauce

Prep:

Mix all ingredients together and spread into a 9x12 pan.

Bake for 30 minutes at 350 degrees.

Put it in a crock pot to keep it warm.

Serve it up:

Serve with celery, crackers, chips, etc.

Did you know that both the hot dog on a bun and the hamburger were introduced to the world at the 1904 St. Louis World's Fair?

It's a Long Distance Love Affair

Life intervenes, teams move, heroes are traded, or loyalties shift.

Sometimes, a person just feels like they were born in the wrong place.

It's a phenomenon that's hard to explain, but it is more common than you would imagine. These people, who travel great distances and stand, sometimes alone, in support of their Team — they are the Mighty, the Misunderstood... they are the Misplaced Fans.

continued (more love)...

Barbecue--St. Louis Style!

In a city that has a style of ribs actually named for it, you'd expect to find a few nice racks around the tailgating lot. So when the time arrived for the Taste-off and none of the contenders brought the legendary St. Louis Ribs, we had to wonder, what gives?

Turns out St. Louis isn't so much a style of ribs as it is a cut. The prime, center section on a rack of pork spare ribs is cut into a neat, even strip making for, some say, the best of all worlds. Small, manageable segments with lots of meat and plenty of marbling to keep 'em moist, they cook evenly and are generally cheaper than your baby backs.

Braise 'em, par boil 'em, smoke 'em or just slow cook 'em on the grill... whatever method you like best is just fine. But it seems in St. Louis, you gotta serve 'em with the sauce. And *the* sauce, without question, is Maull's. A St. Louis institution for more than a hundred years, you can't have a barbecue around here without it!

It's also a required ingredient for another local favorite, perhaps less known but possibly even more loved... the St. Louis pork steak. Cut from the center of the pork shoulder, one local described them as "a pork chop from the wrong side of town."

An inexpensive, typically fatty piece of meat, these steaks are grilled--sslloowwllyy-- over an open flame, then smothered in sauce. Yummm!

Smoked Seahawk Salmon Chowder

Blacktop Chef, John Messbarger

Ingredients:

2	med onions, chopped
1 1/2	sticks unsalted butter
1/4	cup flour
1	gallon whole milk
1	pint cream
3	lbs potatoes, cubed
3	lbs fresh salmon fillet
1	lb smoked salmon *(broken into chunks)*
1/2	cup fresh dill, chopped
3	Tbsp cayenne pepper
3	Tbsp hot sauce

Smoked Gouda, shredded

Sliced baguette

Prep:

Make sure you have all your ingredients ready to go before you get to the lot.

Cook:

Sauté the onions in butter in a cast iron Dutch oven. Add the flour, milk, cream and potatoes. Bring to a boil.

Turn the heat down and simmer for 20 minutes until the potatoes are tender.

Add the fresh salmon to the Dutch oven and simmer for 5 minutes. Remove the salmon and break into small chunks.

Return the cooked salmon chunks to the chowder and add smoked salmon, dill, cayenne pepper and hot sauce. Let simmer for at least 30 minutes.

Serve it up:

Sprinkle the Gouda cheese over the top and serve with sliced baguette.

Wow factor!

Use hollowed-out sourdough rolls to serve your chowder in.

St. Louis Rams

More Love...

In St. Louis, we tailgated with a huge group from the *Midwest Seahawkers* for their annual Ambush at the Arch. More than a hundred members strong, they travel to Seahawks games across the country. And they're not alone!

The Rampagers are a group of loyal Rams fans from around the globe who get together online and at tailgating events. The Eagles have their *Floridelphians*, and there are *Packer Backers* everywhere from Memphis to Seattle, Tulsa to Tampa.

And New Orleans... well, they've got a bunch of crazy Brits who call themselves the *British Saints*. They actually fly to New Orleans for several games every year!

These fans prove that with enough passion and devotion, love *can* survive across the miles.

DETROIT LIONS

The Pride of Lions

Sometimes a stadium is more than a stadium. Sometimes it's a symbol of success (Seattle), sometimes it's a statement of love (Green Bay), and sometimes, as in Detroit, it's an act of urban reclamation.

In 2002, the Lions made the move from the suburbs into downtown Detroit, in a calculated attempt to revive a blighted city. Many feared their great tailgating tradition would be stomped by city ordinances restricting the use of open flames in the civic center, but the city made accommodations and has even established an official tailgating lot with reasonable rates at the nearby Eastern Market. It's about a ten-minute walk from the stadium, but then again, that's part of the urban experience.

When fans come into the city and interact with each other, experience new things and discover new places, they begin to think of the city as their own. Ford Field has given Detroit back their Lions, and now the Pride will only continue to grow.

Blacktop's Best...

Nightmare Chili

Blacktop Chef, John Armaly III

"Where did the cowboys first cook up their chili? Off the backs of their wagons! That sounds like the original tailgate dish to me. That's why I make it. I only use pure and simple ingredients. No B.S. You won't find any wussy beans or girly tomatoes in this chili! It's called 'Johnny's Nightmare' because after you eat it, you go to bed warm and cozy... and wake up in the darkest part of hell!"

Johnny and his tailgating pals T-Bone, Wolfman, Rash and Snake have the right attitude, and stomach, for this tasty chili!

"We've had it on everything from eggs to burgers. The best way to eat it is straight up. Grab on tight and feel the burn!"

-John Armaly III

Ingredients:

1	large white onion
1	medium yellow or sweet onion, chopped
7-8	cloves garlic, coarsely chopped
1	lb ground lamb
1	lb ground beef
1	lb ground pork
6 1/2	lbs cubed beef roast
1	Tbsp cumin
2	poblano chiles, chopped
4	Hungarian chiles, chopped
16	habanero chiles, chopped
4-6	serrano chiles
1	can chiles packed in adobo sauce
15	oz beef broth
3-4	beers

Salt to taste

White corn tortilla chips

Prep and Cook:

1 Day Before:

In a large cast iron Dutch oven, sweat onion for 5 to 7 minutes. Do not brown! Add garlic and sweat for 5 more minutes. Remove onion and garlic mix from oven and set aside.

A little at a time, brown all the meat in the same oven. Add the onion and garlic back to the pot once all the meat is browned. Add cumin and stir for 1 to 2 minutes.

Add all the chiles (coarsely chopped, with most of the seeds removed), broth, beer and salt. Simmer for 5 hours on low.

"I like Porters, but whatever's in the fridge!"

Let it cool and refrigerate overnight.

Game Day:

Put Dutch oven on grill and warm up the chili. Once it's warm, add tortilla chips to thicken the chili to desired consistency. Mix well and let simmer for 2 more hours. Stir frequently.

Serve it up:

Eat it straight from a bowl or on your favorite food and enjoy the heat.

You don't know beans...

...about chili, if you think that they belong in it! That's what John Armaly (and pretty much any citizen of the entire state of Texas) will tell you if you try to slip some pintos into your pot.

You see, while every region of the country seems to have their own style of chili — heck, most places these days you can even find the VEGETARIAN varieties — the original concoction, the stuff cooked up on wagon trains all across the West, was made from meat, chiles, and little else.

Range cooks would actually plant herb gardens along the trails, with garlic, onions, chiles, oregano, and comino. They'd harvest what they needed and toss it into a pot with whatever they managed to kill that day... jackrabbit, rattlesnake, buffalo or beef, it really didn't matter. They'd simmer it up in a cast iron pot over an open campfire — hearty, easy, and hot!

Today, creative cooks throw in everything from coffee to corn, beer and even peanuts!

XL Treatment

Detroit has been revitalized, and Harry's Bar is one of the reasons why. Located just a few blocks from Comerica and Ford Field, Harry's boasts good food and great service.

Team Blacktop and the Tour Coach decided to hang with Harry and his gang for their Extra Large Super Bowl Party, and we had a great time meeting all the Steelers' and Seahawks' fans. See you next year in Miami!

"This place is just cool to hang out. Totally mixed crowd, which is unusual in Detroit. The food is upscale bar food and you don't have to deal with $12 martinis."

-Matthew

Storm's Motor City Kitty's Steak Sandwiches

Blacktop Chef, Mike Sandstrom

These beauties were gone almost as soon as they were brought over. Mike makes these because "they are minimal prep... easy to make... which leaves more time for fun at the tailgate."

Ingredients:

1	**green bell pepper**
1	**red bell pepper**
1	**large white onion**
1	**lb deli-sliced roast beef** *(1 lb for every 2 people)*
2	**Tbsp Worcestershire sauce**
1	**Tbsp Heinz 57** *(or favorite steak sauce)*

Deli sliced provolone cheese

Non-stick cooking spray

Buns or rolls

Prep:

Slice the peppers and onion. Sauté peppers and onion in the non-stick cooking spray. Add beef, Worcestershire and Heinz 57.

Remove from heat and marinate overnight in fridge.

Grill:

Use a skillet or griddle on your grill and warm the beef, onion and pepper mix.

Slice your buns or rolls and toast.

Serve it up:

Put a generous portion of the beef, onion and peppers on a bun and top with provolone cheese. You'll need at least 2 napkins to eat this!

Carnitas de Castillo

Team Blacktop's
Lenny and Nikki

The Castillos flew in and grilled up two roasts that were devoured by everyone at the Detroit tailgate.

Ingredients:

1   4-6 lb pork butt

Kosher salt

Granulated garlic

Fresh cracked pepper

Ground cumin

Tecate beer

2-3   limes, cut into wedges

Tortillas

Prep:

Rub seasonings on roast and place on rotisserie spit. Drink a Tecate with lime.

Heat the grill to 400 degrees. Drink a Tecate with lime.

Rotisserie:

Put the rotisserie on the grill and cook for 15 minutes. Turn the heat down to medium. Drink a Tecate with lime.

Use Tecate to put out any flames, and drink a Tecate with lime. (Use an aluminum roasting pan underneath the pork to catch any juices. This also helps with flare-ups and scorch marks.)

Squeeze lime on the pork as it cooks. Drink a Tecate with lime.

Roast is done when meat thermometer reads 160 degrees. Drink Tecate with lime.

Serve it up:

Shred pork and serve with condiments: avocado, cilantro, scallions, chopped olives, sour cream and Frank's RedHot Chile n Lime. Pile your pork and sides onto a warm tortilla and enjoy with a Tecate and lime. See Stella's Tortillas for *the best* homemade tortillas.

Stella's Tortillas

Blacktop Chef, Stella Castillo

Ingredients:

3   cups La Pina flour

1   tsp salt

1/4   cup lard

1/2   cup warm water

Prep & Grill:

Place flour, lard and salt in a large bowl. Blend with a pastry blender or two knives until crumbly, about 3 to 5 minutes. Gradually add warm water and continue kneading until dough is smooth, about 3 minutes. Divide dough into 12 pieces. Rub your hands with a little lard then roll dough into a ball and place on a baking tray. Cover with a towel and let rest at room temperature for 15 - 60 minutes. Lightly flour a cutting board and roll out each ball into a tortilla. Cook on a heated griddle until it begins to bubble, turn and repeat on other side.

PHILADELPHIA EAGLES

Can you feel the love?

Philly tailgaters have got the best of both worlds; the proximity and energy of a stadium in the heart of a great city, plus the roomy parking lots associated with much more suburban locations.

"The Linc" is part of a sprawling sports complex less than four miles from downtown. Plentiful, cheap parking encourages one of the liveliest tailgating communities around, and these loyal fans come out to party in sunshine or in snow, in fleets of often-vintage tailgating vehicles.

Although finding a bar that's stumbling distance from the stadium can be a trick (there *is* McFadden's)-- really, who needs to when you've got friendly, fun-loving Philly fans with their amazing Margaritas and coolers full of Yuengling?

Philadelphia is, without a doubt, one of those cities that makes you love to call America home.

And Philadelphia is full of football fans who love to call the Eagles their team.

Blacktop's Best...
Eric's 'Zoned Out' Surf-n-Turf

Blacktop Chef, Eric Mitchell

There are tailgaters, and then there are tailgate crews. Tailgaters bring out food and drink to enjoy in the parking lot before the game. Crews like *Zoned Out*, they set up the giant inflatables, have nicknames like PJ Boy and Urinator, and haul fully equipped utility trailers complete with spice racks (???).

When this crew rolls into the lot, the message is clear: We're Philly fans and the party is HERE!

Ingredients:

Salmon fillet

Porterhouse steak

Jumbo shrimp

Little neck clams and mussels

2   sticks of butter

5-6   lemons

Steak rub

Salmon seasoning

Shrimp, Clam and Mussel seasoning

Non-stick cooking spray

Prep:

Prep the rub and seasonings in Zoned Out's Spice Rack *(see recipes this page)*. Combine the ingredients and store in labeled containers.

Grill:

Steak:

Heat grill to medium heat. Spray both sides of the steak with cooking spray, and rub both sides with steak rub. Cook steaks for 9 minutes on one side, then turn over and cook for 7 minutes on the other side for medium rare.

Salmon:

Place a piece of tin foil down on the table. Put 6-7 tabs of butter on the foil and place salmon fillet on top. Put 6-7 more tabs of butter on top of the salmon. Cut a lemon in half and squeeze over the salmon. Spread the salmon seasoning over the fish and wrap the foil over the salmon to seal it in. Cook over medium heat, turning several times until fish is cooked through.

Mussels and Clams:

Shuck mussels and clams and place, in half shells, on a high heat grill. Squeeze lemon and sprinkle Clam and Mussel seasoning over the tops. Grill for 2 minutes.

Shrimp:

Place 6 shrimp on a skewer and spray with cooking spray. Sprinkle shrimp seasoning over the shrimp. Cook for 3 minutes on each side.

Serve it up:

If you have to use a plate, go ahead!

Zoned Out Spice Rack

Steak rub:

1	Tbsp black pepper
1	Tbsp Mrs. Dash
1	Tbsp salt
1/2	Tbsp Old Bay

Salmon seasoning:

1	Tbsp sea salt
1	Tbsp Old Bay
1	tsp black pepper
1	Tbsp Emeril's Essence
2	Tbsp Montreal seasoning

Shrimp, Clam and Mussel seasoning:

2 1/2	Tbsp Old Bay
2	Tbsp Emeril's Essence
1/2	Tbsp Montreal seasoning
1	Tbsp salt
1	Tbsp pepper
1/2	Tbsp Frank's Hot Sauce

Maniac Margarita

Ingredients:

Cuervo 1800

Roses Lime Juice

Triple Sec

Cointreau Orange Liqueur

Sweet and sour mix

Lime

Margarita salt

How to:

"Make sure that Margarita is salted in a lovely red plastic cup!"

Fill cup with ice and mix 1-1/2 ounces Cuervo 1800 with 3/4 ounce Triple Sec, 3/4 ounce Cointreau. Stir. Fill with sweet and sour mix and add lime juice to top. Stir well and enjoy!

Jim's Jammin' Jambalaya

Blacktop Chef, Jim Kay

Ingredients:

4	boxes Zatarain's jambalaya mix
8	cloves garlic, chopped
4	small jalapenos, chopped
4	red peppers, chopped
4	green peppers, chopped
2	onions, chopped
4	cups celery, chopped
1	lb large, shrimp, peeled
1	lb chicken, diced
1	lb hot sausage, cut into pieces
1	lb sweet sausage, cut into pieces
2	cans Yuengling Lager

Wishbone Italian dressing

Texas Pete Hot Sauce

Salt, pepper, garlic and onion powder

Crushed red pepper

Creole seasoning

Olive oil

"Our jambalaya not only tastes the best, but it has the same 'kick' the Eagles have. It's just the perfect combination of meats, spices, rices and seasonings. Not only will our Jambalaya keep you warm, it will leave you with a huge-ass smile on your face!"

Prep:

Marinate chicken, shrimp, hot & sweet sausage in beer, hot sauce, salt, pepper, Creole seasoning, Italian dressing, garlic powder and onion powder for approx. 1 hour (the longer the better).

Cook:

Cook each of the meats until they are halfway done (they will finish cooking in the pot).

In a large Dutch oven, add olive oil. When hot, add garlic, onions, jalapenos, celery, crushed red pepper and fresh red/green peppers. Sauté for a few minutes. Add water (amount on Zatarain's box) and bring to a boil.

Add contents of rice packet and stir until you reach a boil. Add meats to the mix. Cover pot and reduce heat to low. Cook approximately 30-40 minutes. Bang!

Serve it up:

"Serve in a plastic dish with a plastic spoon. Eat it like you're at a tailgate with a Maniac Margarita!"

Famous Philly Foods...

Strolling through the tailgating lots in Philadelphia, a unique smell hangs in the early morning air. Breakfast is sizzling on skillets everywhere, and around here, breakfast means SCRAPPLE.

I wrinkled my nose at the grayish loaf, sliced thin and frying in oil. "What's in it?" was, of course, the obvious question. The answer: "You probably don't want to know."

An invention of the notoriously frugal Pennsylvania Dutch, scrapple blends pork scraps and offals with cornmeal mush and spices. The result is something like SPAM, and is often served covered in ketchup or maple syrup. (We had ours with a few dashes of Frank's RedHot Sauce, and it wasn't half bad!)

Another Philly favorite of questionable origin is the pork roll. Native only to the Philadelphia-Trenton region, pork rolls are typically sliced and served on a breakfast sandwich with egg and cheese. Something akin to a ham, it has a tangier taste and is always ordered by name. Recipes will call for Taylor Pork Roll or Case Pork Roll, depending on what neighborhood the cook is from.

And then, of course, there's the Cheesesteak, whose tempting scent wafts through the city from street vendors' carts. Traditionally, thin slices of grilled steak are chopped and served on an Amoroso Roll with white American cheese or Cheez Whiz. Often grilled onions, sautéed peppers and mushrooms are offered as options, but purists scoff at such embellishments.

Yuengling... Your Beer is Calling!

Get anywhere even close to Pennsylvania and you can hear a distinctive ring in the air. No, it's not the sound of freedom, echoing through history. It's the sound of beer lovers calling for the mid-Atlantic's finest!

Yuengling (rhymes with ring-ring) is a local favorite that has been brewed in Pottsville, Pennsylvania since 1829.

America's Oldest Brewery, it was opened originally as Eagle Brewery and the label still bears the image of a majestic bald eagle.

A smooth, full-bodied lager, is it any wonder this is the beer of choice at any Philly tailgate?

Breakfast... in a Bag?

Blacktop Chef, Steven Rickershauser

This is a great recipe for those early morning tailgates. Prep it all the night before, and clean-up is a snap!

Ingredients:

Zippered freezer bags, qt. sized

Eggs, raw scrambled

Ham, diced

Onions, diced

Bell peppers, diced

Olives, chopped

Mushrooms, chopped

Cheese, shredded

Prep:

Dice, chop, scramble and shred everything the night before. Store each ingredient in separate sealed containers and keep as cold as possible until ready to cook.

Cook:

Bring a large pot of water to a boil.

Each person takes a zipper bag, adds a scoop* of eggs, and any other ingredients they want. Drop bags into pot and boil for 10 minutes. Remove with tongs, unzip, and empty onto plate. Enjoy!

*(1 scoop = 2 raw eggs = 1/2 cup)

54

Team Blacktop Tip:

Try making this breakfast in a Camp Chef Cooking Iron instead of a bag. Just add the ingredients to the iron and close. Hold over an open flame until done.

Kick-Ass Chicken Legs

Blacktop Chef, John Ianelli

An aspiring chef at 17, John could teach even seasoned veterans a thing or two about tailgating. Forget wimpy wings, this dish has a taste so big, only drum sticks will do. Nice legs, John!

Ingredients:

Chicken legs, full size

McCormick's Grill Mates Italian Seasoning

Frank's Original RedHot Sauce

Oregano, ground

Salt and pepper

Prep:

Combine Italian seasoning and Frank's. Mix well and brush on chicken. Sprinkle chicken with oregano, salt and pepper.

Cook:

Cook chicken on a medium heat grill until done.

Serve it up:

Grab and go...

Gorgonzola Burgers

Blacktop Chef, Mike Knowland

This is one of only two burgers to make the book. It's the combination of the tangy marinade and the Gorgonzola cheese that make this burger one of Blacktop's Best!

Ingredients:

16   sirloin burgers
(hint: use prepared patties)

1/2   cup soy sauce

1/2   cup Moore's Marinade

Several shakes of Worcestershire

Montreal steak seasoning

Gorgonzola cheese, crumbled

Olive oil

Focaccia rolls

The prepared sirloin burgers tend to hold up better in the marinade.

Prep:

In a mixing bowl, combine soy sauce, Moore's, Worcestershire and Montreal seasoning. Marinate the burgers overnight.

Cook:

Put the burgers on the grill and cook as desired. Melt the crumbled Gorgonzola over the burgers.

Brush olive oil on focaccia and toast on the grill.

Serve it up:

Serve as is or add your favorite burger toppings.

Caribe Pork

Blacktop Chef, Mike Knowland

Ingredients:

1   3-4 lb pork tenderloin

1   bottle Goya Mojo marinade

Olive oil

1 lg sweet onion, sliced

Frank's Original RedHot Sauce

Provolone cheese, sliced

Rolls

Prep and Cook:

2 Days Before:

Cut pork in half and place each half in a freezer bag. Add onion and marinade. Place in refrigerator overnight.

1 Day Before:

Pour about 2 ounces of olive oil in a cast iron Dutch oven and add pork and contents of freezer bag. Cook at 300 degrees for about 6 hours. The pork is done when you can shred it easily with a fork.

Shred pork and add Frank's to your desired level of heat. Refrigerate overnight.

Game Day:

Warm in Dutch oven on grill and serve on roll with cheese.

Keep in mind... Oversized parking can be pricey! We've paid anywhere from $40 to $400!

56

Tricked out Tailgating!

Fans show team pride with their pimped out rides...

If, when you think of tailgating, you picture styrofoam coolers and hibachis in the bed of a pickup truck, you haven't been tailgating lately. Seems these days, fans are going to extremes to create the ultimate parking lot parties, and they begin with their rigs.

Beat-up busses and retired RVs are popular choices, as they offer plenty of room for the whole crew. Fanatics paint them up in their team colors and outfit them with all the conveniences of home. Couches, kitchens, toilets and TVs are common. Some have built-in bars, and others, like the Bohemian Party Vessel in DC, take the fun to new heights with their roof decks.

Others opt for delivery trucks, which are great for hauling out tons of tailgating gear. Big Blue BBQ packs theirs full of the grills, coolers, tents, tables, and portable heaters they use to set up a small tailgating village!

And Keith and Liz turned their legendary BlueBird into a living room on wheels, with wood paneling, upholstered benches, and TWO televisions -- one to watch the Giants, and one to watch the Eagles, of course!

We saw utility trailers with custom graphics, built out with bars, and sporting flat panel TVs!

In Arizona, our neighbors were partying in a jacked-up 4x4 monster truck limousine. In San Francisco, they were tailgating on the deck of an old 1968 fire engine.

One of our favorites was the Falcon Fanbulance in Atlanta, a rig fully equipped and ready to respond to any tailgating emergency.

Seahawk fans were servin' it up from a killer tailgating trailer, with a built-in grill, complete kitchen and beer taps! A lot like a party boat on wheels, the other end has upholstered bench seating all around.

These tailgating rigs have many advantages, like being able to load them up with all your gear just once for the whole season.

And they also have their disadvantages, like being a magnet for every woman who's afraid to use the port-a-johns.

If you're thinking of crossing that line into obsessive tailgating, but want to try it out first, you can always rent an RV for the weekend!

Companies like El Monte RV often offer tailgating packages. They'll stock it up and even deliver it to your spot, so all you have to do is show up and party!

NEW YORK GIANTS

BIG Time Tailgating!

Around the Big Apple, they like to do things BIG. Big buildings, big business, big attitude...

And BIG tailgating for the Big Blue.

The Giants have plenty of BIG fans! They drive BIG fanmobiles and haul out BIG smoker trailers to the BIG tailgating lots around Giants stadium. They cook up BIG racks of ribs (we think Brontosaurus!) and throw out a BIG New York "welcome."

We're not kidding.

When we pulled into this tailgating lot, as the dawn blushed pink over the Manhattan skyline, our neighbors actually stopped what they were doing to come over and help us unload!

All day, we were treated like guests in the home of good friends. Our glass never empty, our stomachs always full, and by the end of the day we were dancing to Sinatra with the biggest of the big, our new friends from the award-winning crew of Big Blue BBQ.

Blacktop's Best...
Austin's Flank Steak

Blacktop Chef, Austin Bregman

Austin was the youngest tailgater to be named Blacktop's Best at only 10! With his avid love of sports, the fact that he is a 3rd generation diehard Giants fan, and his ability to throw down the smack, this kid is New York to the CORE!

"The Giants have a reputation for devoted fans passing along the tradition from generation to generation. Being the youngest competitor to win, and having it be on the day Wellington Mara was honored, makes October 30th a lifetime memory. Go Big Blue!"

Ingredients:

Flank steak

Dry Rub:

   Blackening seasoning

   Granulated garlic

   Salt and Pepper

Soy sauce

Teriyaki sauce

Prep:

2 Days Before

Rub blackening seasoning, garlic, salt and pepper on flank steaks. Put steaks in resealable freezer bag and add the soy and teriyaki sauce. Add just enough to get the steak wet. Marinate for 48 hours.

Cook:

Game Day:

Heat grill to medium heat. Put steaks in a foil packet and place on grill. Put leftover marinade in foil packet and close. Cook until done.

Serve it up:

Slice and serve the flank steak over a bed of roasted garlic, sweet peppers and sharp provolone cheese and/or put on a roll to make an awesome sandwich.

Rack o' Lamb a la Beast

Blacktop Chef, Michael Rinaldo

Ingredients:

1	New Zealand rack of lamb
1	cup Gulden's mustard
1/4	cup minced garlic
1	tsp pepper
1	tsp salt
1/2	cup breadcrumbs
1/2	cup mint jelly

Prep:

Rub lamb with mustard then rub with minced garlic. Add salt and pepper. Roll in breadcrumbs.

Cook:

Roast or smoke until done.

Serve it up:

Serve with mint jelly and fresh grilled bell peppers.

Code Blue BBQ

Blacktop Chef, Jonathan Zisa

"In this day and age of weight watching and health-food nuts, we like to go back to the times of clogging arteries, living life to the fullest, and having a good time. In essence, if you can't have a good time eating and being with friends, you should not be anywhere near a tailgate, or even be considered for being one of Blacktop's Best!"

-Jonathan Zisa

The fun loving EMTs from Code Blue BBQ aren't joking when they say, "If you're feeling chest pain, look for the nearest EMT or call 911." The breakfast and lunch they serve up is enough to clog the Hudson River!

Heart Attack Breakfast

Ingredients:

Eggs

Taylor pork roll

Maple-cured bacon

Cheese *(to your liking)*

Condiments

(ketchup, mustard, mayo, etc.)

Salt and pepper to taste

Fresh bakery hard roll

Prep and Grill:

On a flat griddle, over medium heat place (per person) 1 egg, 2 strips of bacon, 1 slice of pork. Cook egg over easy, bacon until just crisp and pork until just golden. Approximately 10 seconds before done, place cheese on egg, layer with ham and bacon.

Serve it up:

Serve hot on a hard roll with condiments of your choice.

The Cardiac Burger

Ingredients:

3	lbs 80% lean ground beef
3	eggs
1	box Lipton's "beefy onion" soup mix
1	cup Worcestershire sauce
2	Tbsp A.1. steak sauce

Taylor pork roll

Maple-cured bacon

Sharp cheddar cheese

Prep and Grill:

Mix ground beef, eggs, Worcestershire, A.1. and 2 packets soup mix by folding in ground beef around it. Gently press patties to desired thickness and size. Cook patty on grill over medium heat until done. Cook bacon until crisp and pork until golden.

Serve it up:

Zisa says that A.1. ketchup, BBQ sauce, pickles and salt and pepper are a MUST!

Beef Wellington Mara

Blacktop Chef, Greg Friedman

On October 30, 2006, the Giants beat the Redskins in one of the oldest rivalries in pro football. It was a fitting tribute to the great Wellington Mara! Greg combined one of the classiest dishes with a little ingenuity to make a good day into an unforgettable one.

"You asked for the best... now you've got it. Sincere blessings to Wellington Mara. Rest in peace!"

-Greg Friedman

Ingredients:

3 packs bacon

2 packs mushrooms, sliced

2 large onions, sliced

2 cups red wine

2 packages phyllo dough

4 sticks butter, melted

8 lbs strip beef loin, cut 3/4 inch thick

Prep, Grill and Serve:

Cook bacon so it is still pliable, but cooked through. Sear steaks for 2 minutes on each side in bacon grease. Sauté mushrooms and onions in bacon grease, add red wine and reduce mixture by half.

Layer 6 phyllo dough squares with melted butter brushed between each layer (8x8 inch squares).

Layer 1 strip of bacon, 1 slice of steak, another strip of bacon, and then top with Wellington mix (mushroom and onion).

Wrap with dough and bake at 400 degrees for 20 minutes.

Use a Dutch oven with rack inside and keep a careful eye on the temperature! Or, bake at home and warm on the grill.

Sandwich-sized for easy eating. Serve with plenty of napkins!

Simply... 'The Duke'

For devoted Giants fans, the blue skies of the October day were clouded only by the recent loss of their team's owner, the Patriarch of the NFL, Wellington Mara.

The son of Giants founder Timothy Mara, he had devoted his whole life to the team. From his days as a ballboy during their first season back in 1925, until his death from cancer in 2005 at the age of 89, Mara served the Giants with a brand of integrity that earned him respect league-wide.

His induction into the Pro Football Hall of Fame in 1997 made the Maras the first father and son with that honor.

He is often quoted for having said, "there are no ex-Giants, only old Giants."

His mark on the sport will be lasting.

Following his death, NFL clubs unanimously voted to rename the official NFL Game Ball "The Duke" in his memory.

"Wellington Mara represented the heart and soul of the National Football League. He was a man of deep conviction who stood as a beacon of integrity."
-Paul Tagliabue

Clam Dip

Blacktop Chef, Kevin Johnson

Ingredients:

6 cloves garlic, chopped

1 large onion, chopped

1 tsp parsley

1 tsp oregano

2 cans minced clams

4 dashes Frank's RedHot

1 Tbsp pepper

1 Tbsp red pepper

1/2 stick butter, melted

1 tsp lemon juice

1/2 cup breadcrumbs

grated cheese

Prep and Cook:

Sauté onions and garlic with butter, add all the spices. Simmer for 10 minutes. In a separate pan, sauté the clams with lemon juice. Simmer for 10 minutes. Mix all the ingredients. Add the breadcrumbs and put in a casserole dish. Top with grated cheese and bake at 400 degrees for 20-25 minutes.

Serve:

Serve with chips or crackers.

Frenchy's South Tailgate Pork

Blacktop Chef, Mike Marino

"There is no better pork on earth!"

Ingredients:

10 1 inch thick boneless pork cutlets

8 cloves garlic, roughly chopped

1 bottle Wishbone Robusto Italian dressing

1 bottle Thai ginger dressing

Basil, garlic powder & black pepper

10 Italian rolls

Prep:

1 Day Before

Make marinade by combining Italian dressing, Thai Ginger dressing, basil, garlic powder, and black pepper in large mixing bowl.

Layer pork cutlets in large resealable container, and pierce them many times with knife.

Rub in chopped garlic, pressing some into slits in pork. Pour marinade over pork, refrigerate overnight.

Grill and Serve:

Game Day:

Grill both sides of pork over high flame until browned.

Butterfly, then grill open faced until browned. Serve pork on Italian roll.

Top Ten Tailgating Tricks & Tips

Everyone knows the right tools make any job easier, and the right toys can put your tailgate over the top! Here are a few ideas that we borrowed from the best:

1. The first thing every great tailgate party needs is a great tailgating cookbook, with tips and recipes from the Blacktop's Best... hey look, you've got one!

2. Remember, tents and tarps can save the day by providing shelter from the rain and wind! Keeping a grill lit can be a real challenge in a gusty spot like the Meadowlands.

3. There's no substitute for a good, sturdy table. You never have enough space for prepping and serving food, and wobbly legs can send your tasty treats tumbling onto the blacktop, and you to the hospital with a nasty cut or burn.

4. Space heaters can be your best friend, or find you a few new ones! Especially when you realize, to quote the boys from Big Blue, "that not only was it windy, it was BEEP-ing cold." We loved our portable campfire from Camp Chef for just this reason. It kept us (and all our tailgating neighbors) warm even on a snowy morning in Green Bay!

5. Water is scarce in a parking lot, which can make clean-up a bit tricky. Minimize the need to wash by using disposable pans, plates, and serving platters whenever possible. Zippered plastic storage bags are a tailgater's best friend! Use them to marinate, organize, store and dispose.

6. Store your stuff in rubber tubs all season long, and avoid the need to pack and repack for each game.

7. Keep hot foods hot in disposable aluminum roasting pans with sterno cans beneath.

8. Keep cold foods cold by filling the lid of one of your tubs with ice from the cooler. Place bowls of salad, trays of cheese, condiments, beverages, or whatever in this instant ice table.

9. A portable, modular cooking system will allow you to grill, boil, fry, bake, steam, or sauté all with the same basic set-up. Versatility means the ability to be more creative!

10. Use large, inflatable novelties or high-flying flags to show your team spirit AND help your guests find you (when word gets out, you WILL have guests!)

GREEN BAY PACKERS

Backers Love Their Packers

The Green Bay Packers got their name from the very first Packer Backers. The Indian Packing Company put up the cash to get the team going, then virtually disappeared from the playing field before the first down.

But the name stuck, and the town stuck by the team, and the fans stuck around, through good times and bad, to watch them grow into one of the greatest success stories in professional sports. Around the world, the name "Green Bay" is synonymous with the Packers -- a football franchise of the fans, by the fans, and for the fans.

The only publicly held team in the NFL, their fans are their owners and they love to boast of the Packers enviable Championship record.

But what they are most proud of is their unparalleled community support. Packer games have been sold out since the '60s, and families are known to put their children's names on the waiting list for season tickets when they are born!

Blacktop's Best...
Smucker's BBQ Raccoon

Blacktop Chef, Steve Muck

Steve and the "Fourth and Twenty-sixers" are found at every Packer game at Lambeau. Steve is an avid cook and owns the Woodland Supper Club in Gresham, WI. Careful when you order, it might be raccoon!

"You need a couple of good coon hounds, a good light, a .22 caliber rifle, a sharp knife and some corn fields. After the dogs tree the coon, you get it out of the tree, skin it, and keep the 4 legs. The fun is over, and the work begins."

Ingredients:

25-30 raccoon legs
(so it's more than one night of fun)

1   **large onion, diced**

1   **clove of garlic, diced**

1   **tsp Jamaican Jerk seasoning**

Salt and Pepper to taste

1   **cup water**

1   **cup red wine**

Lawry's Seasoned Salt to taste

Plenty   Windsor and Sun-Drop
(for the cook)

12   **oz mushrooms, diced**

1   **large bottle BBQ sauce**

Prep and Cook:

1 Day Before:

Clean ALL the fat off the legs. Cut all the meat off the bones and place into a cast iron Dutch oven on the grill. Add the water, wine, all the seasonings, the mushrooms and about 1 cup of BBQ sauce. (By now you should be on the 3rd or 4th Windsor and Sun-Drop!) Roast at 300 for 3-4 hours. Let cool and drain all the juices. Shred meat.

Game Day:

Return meat to Dutch oven and add the rest of the BBQ sauce. Simmer on low until ready to eat.

Serve it up:

Serve on fresh potato buns or hard rolls.

"Have some great Wisconsin cheese! I like 3 to 5 year old Cheddar, potato salad on the side, more Windsor or your favorite cocktail, 15 to 20 of your friends, assorted stories and jokes, and don't forget to kiss the cook!"
-Steve Muck

If you didn't get a chance to go 'coon huntin' and you're fresh out, this recipe is very versatile. You can use shredded chicken, beef or pork instead of the raccoon. Be sure to garnish your plate with plenty of cheese, from Wisconsin, of course!

Brats 101

Bratwurst, from the German *braten* meaning roasted or fried, and *wurst* meaning sausage, is a raw encased meat traditionally made from pork, and sometimes beef or veal.

In 'sconsin, they're usually grilled and served on a bun with mustard, grilled onions, and/or sauerkraut, (and beer, of course!) and every cheesehead swears that his brats are the best!

Because bratwurst are raw, unlike hot dogs or smoked sausages, it's best to cook them in some sort of two-step manner to avoid under-cooking the inside or scorching the skin.

- **Grill 'em till golden over the flames, then move them to a cooler spot on the grill to cook through.**

- **Simmer them stovetop in light liquid before moving them onto the grill.**

- **Brown in a cast iron skillet, then turn down the heat and put a lid on until done.**

Remember the rule:

Pork should never be pink!

Blacktop Brats

Team Blacktop's Jay

The influences of German immigrants still flavor most aspects of life throughout the Midwest. And nowhere are they more apparent than in the love affair between Wisconsin cheeseheads, their beer, and their brats.

In fact, this tasty tube-meat is so much a part of their culture that it is almost taken for granted, dismissed as ordinary.

Time after time, as we worked our way through the tailgating lots around Lambeau asking "so what's on the grill today?" we were met with a shrug and an almost apologetic, "Oh, just brats."

But the sausages Packer fans pull off their grills are far from ordinary! We picked up a few tips from their best Blacktop Chefs about how to cook and serve up brats tasty enough to impress even a lifelong Packer fan.

Ingredients:

Olive oil

Large white onions, sliced thin

Bratwurst

Six-pack Blonde Ale

Spicy mustard

Fresh rolls

Simmer:

In a cast iron Dutch oven, cover bottom with olive oil and put onion slices to cover the bottom. Place brats on onion and cover with Ale.

Turn grill on to medium-high heat and poach brats for 30-45 minutes. Be careful not to let the beer completely evaporate.

Grill:

Remove brats and place directly on grill grate. Brown all sides.

In a Dutch oven, let the beer reduce to a thick syrup and add just enough mustard to change the color to yellow. Sauté onion until brats are done.

Serve it up:

Serve brats on rolls with onions piled high. Add a touch of mustard.

It's the Cheesiest!

Wisconsin is undeniably the cheesiest place in America (if not the WORLD). And we mean that in a good way. I mean, who doesn't LOVE cheese?

Cheese is an essential element of any Packer's tailgate (in fact, we noticed that it garnished EVERY dish in the Taste-off). So here's a quick guide to help you venture beyond sliced American.

Easy, cheesy, beautiful...

To add a touch of class to your tailgate, serve cubes of soft Farmer's cheese with crunchy smoked almonds and a fruity wine.

Fresh cheese curds are hugely popular in 'sconsin, though they may be impossible to find elsewhere. If you're lucky enough to get your hands on some, they're a salty, squeaky, tailgating delight. Pop 'em straight while enjoying one of Milwaukee's finest... bet you can't eat just one. Or, if you really hate your arteries, how 'bout trying them deep fried!

Toss chunks of Mozzarella and fresh tomato in a zesty Italian dressing for a quick, easy, and irresistible salad.

Nikki likes to sip her wine with a nice slice of Parmesan dipped in honey.

Like it stinky? Wisconsin is one of the only places you can find Beer Cheese, a pungent cousin of Limburger, often dunked into beer before eaten!

Cheese is a versatile ingredient that has found it's way into every imaginable type of food. You can stir it into soups, stuff it into meat, or melt it on top of a nice hot slice of apple pie.

Some like it hot...

Here's a few pointers to keep in mind whenever cheese is on the menu...

Always cook cheese at a low temperature. Intense heat will make it tough and stringy.

Add cheese to soups, sauces, and casseroles near the end to prevent overcooking, which can cause cheese to separate.

Keepin' it fresh...

Hard cheese can stay fresh in the fridge for up to eight weeks, softer cheeses should be used within two. The key is to limit exposure to air. Keep them wrapped up tight in the cooler!

Pre-shredding is a great way to save time at the tailgate, but remember shredded cheeses can dry out and develop mold within a few days.

Beer Cheese Soup

Blacktop Chef, Norma Busch

Ingredients:

1/4	cup flour
1/2	cup butter
2	cups sharp cheddar, shredded
1 1/2	cups half and half
1	Tbsp Worcestershire sauce
3	cups chicken broth, heated
3/4	cup (or more) beer

Music to the ears...

A party just isn't a party without music, and no one knows that better than the tailgaters in Green Bay. Every gameday, they're treated to the festive sounds of the Packer Band -- alternately called the Six Pack -- who wander through the parking lots and streets surrounding the stadium with horns, drums, banjos... and even a washboard.

Cook and Simmer:

Melt butter in pan. Stir in flour, using wire whip. Cook until smooth. Slowly add half and half, stirring constantly. Cook over low heat.

Add chicken broth. Stir in cheddar, Worcestershire sauce, and beer. Stir constantly until cheese is melted through and soup is creamy.

Serve it up:

Serve with fresh roll or in a bread bowl. Make sure you have left over beer!

Hail, hail the gang's all here to yell for you,
And keep you going in your winning ways,
Hail, hail the gang's all here to tell you too,
That win or lose, we'll always sing your
praises, Packers;
Go, you Packers, go and get 'em,
Go, you fighting fools upset 'em,
Smash their line with all your might,
A Touchdown, Packers, Fight, Fight, Fight,
Fight on, you Green and Gold, to glory,
Win this game the same old story,
Fight, you Packers,
Fight, & bring the bacon home to
old Green Bay.

"Wherever you go it's not hard to find someone who would not give up their eye teeth to go to Lambeau Field and feel the tingle on the back of your neck when the Packers hit the field... to ex-perience the tradi-tion and the uncon-ditional love the fans and the state of Wisconsin have for their PACKERS."
-Steve Muck

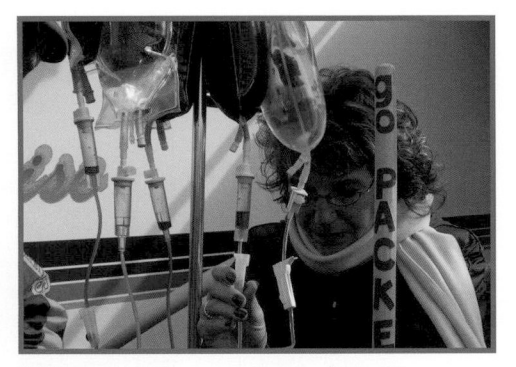

Most Creative Tailgate Set-up...

This award, without question, goes to the crazy Packer fans who pushed around a medical cart stocked with tailgating snacks and hung with IV bags full of booze. All day they rolled through the tailgating lot administering shots and spreading their own unique brand of Packer cheer!

Most Creative Shot on the Spot...

As the "booze cart" made its way to Team Blacktop, we decided to donate some Frank's Red Hot Sauce to the cause. The next thing we knew, they were serving us Bloody Mary SHOTS. 1 olive, vodka and 3-4 shakes of Frank's in a shot glass. Bottoms up!

"The Duffy Miracle!"

1	jar each pickles and olives
2/3	cup vinegar
1 1/2	cups sugar
1/2	cup water
2	tsp 'XXX' horseradish

Prep:

Get yourself a jar of dill pickle spears and a jar of green olives. Combine the two jars into a large jar or container. Add ingredients and let marry for at least a week. The longer, the better!

Most Creative Recipe...

Chuck Brandt's recipe for a great Green Bay tailgate was handwritten, spiraling around the inside of a paper bowl! Though we're not sure exactly what this would taste like, it sounds like a good time!

"Start by killing and processing a deer.

Follow with a cold 12 pack of your favorite Wisconsin lager.

Brown 2 lbs ground beef.

Sauté vegetables taken from your neighbor's garden.

Add the juice of a lot of tomatoes.

Drink another 12 pack.

In the morning, serve with crackers and another 12 pack of beer."

-and cheese, of course!

CHICAGO BEARS

My Kind of Town...

Soldier Field has what could be the most spectacular location in the NFL. Standing tall and proud, between South Lakeshore Drive and the Burnham Marina, it counts as its distinguished neighbors Chicago landmarks like the Shedd Aquarium, Adler Planetarium, and the Field Museum of Natural History.

The world-famous Chicago skyline, featuring the Sears Tower and Chrysler building, forms the backdrop for the Bears games, and Lake Michigan sparkles nearby on a clear autumn day.

Depending on who you talk to, the 2003 remodel of the historic building with its distinctive doric columns was either a brilliant modernization of a cultural icon or "The Mistake on the Lake."

Either way, Bears fans still consider Soldier Field hallowed ground, and often make long pilgrimages to return, game after game.

We met one man who has only missed a single home game since the Bears moved to Soldier Field in 1971, and he lives six hours away in Indiana.

Blacktop's Best...
da Bears Bus Beef

Blacktop Chef, Tim Shanley

Timmy from da Bus pulls into the same spot for every Bears home game. He and tailgating partner Dave have a retrofitted school bus with all the amenities for a great party.

During the warmer games, da Bus tailgates in the lot, as well as on a couple of boats in Burnham Harbor. After a feast at da Bus, a harbor cruise and more great food, Timmy and gang end up at da Bus Stop, where a live band entertains the lot.

It's hard to believe that they have time for a football game!

Ingredients:

1   10 lb inside beef roast

6   garlic cloves, peeled and sliced in half

Olive oil

Salt

Coarse fresh ground pepper

Teriyaki sauce (approx. 7 oz. bottle)

Prep:

1 Day Before:

Using a butcher knife, penetrate the roast 12 times. Try to spread the holes evenly around the roast. Insert a sliced garlic clove deep into each penetration. Place into a large bowl and rub the roast with a light coating of olive oil. Salt and pepper the entire roast evenly.

NOTE: The olive oil helps the salt and pepper cling to the roast.

Pour the entire bottle of teriyaki sauce over the roast. Roll the roast around in the sauce. Try to make sure that teriyaki gets deep into the penetrations in the roast as well. Let the roast marinate over night.

NOTE: Try to roll the roast around every few hours or so if possible.

Rotisserie:

Game Day:

Tie down the roast on your rotisserie. Cook at medium heat until internal temperature is 160 degrees. Discard marinade. This roast should be sliced thinly and served rare/medium rare. If some of your tailgating fans want their roast beef cooked to medium well/well, then just slice the beef at rare and place it on the grill until satisfied.

NOTE: After slicing the outer portions of the roast, you may find that the roast is becoming too rare to eat. Simply brush the roast with another coat of olive oil and add more salt and pepper, and let it cook back up. Since time is of the essence while tailgating, this grilling method allows you to serve the roast a lot quicker.

Serve it up:

Serve with dirty rice and fresh grilled veggies!

Shore Lunch Potatoes

Blacktop Chef, Bill Smith

Ingredients:

Red potatoes, sliced thin

Bell peppers, diced

Onions, diced

Corn Oil

Butter

Cajun Spice

Lemon Pepper

1/3 can condensed milk

Salt and Pepper

Prep and Cook:

In a large cast iron skillet, heat enough oil to cover the bottom of the skillet until hot enough to light a match. (Seriously, stick a match in the oil. If it's hot enough, the match will light-- old Canadian trick!)

Add potatoes, onion and green pepper. Pan fry 10-15 minutes.

Add Cajun spice, lemon pepper, milk, salt and pepper. Pile a couple sticks of butter over the top and let it melt.

Cook, while continually moving ingredients for about 20-25 minutes. Remove from pan and place on a paper towel to soak up drippings.

Have a Seat!

While cruising the lots in search of great food, we discovered that sometimes tailgating lots can look a lot like a flea market.

Seems that items leftover from yard sales often find their way into fans tailgating gear. From old sofas to neon bar lights, carved wooden pigs to macramé lawn chairs, tailgaters outfit their parties with the odd, the interesting, and the unusual.

And two of our favorites belonged to Bears fans. In Chicago, we tailgated next to a group that displays a big, helmeted bear head on their bar at every game. And on the road in Tampa, they were partying with life-sized cutouts of Marilyn Monroe and Walter Payton in old stadium seats!

Bears Baby Back Ribs

Blacktop Chef, Jeanette Weber

Jeanette says that these ribs "melt in your mouth and are finger licking good!" The judges agreed.

Ingredients:

2   **slabs of baby back ribs**

Dry rib rub *(see Kickoff Rub page 10)*

Braising liquid

1 1/2	**cups red wine**
4-5	**Tbsp Worcestershire**
1/2	**cup honey**
3	**Tbsp vinegar**
1/2	**tsp garlic powder**

1   **large onion, sliced**

6   **cloves garlic, sliced**

Prep:

1 Day Before:

Remove membrane from ribs. Generously rub both sides with rib rub. Wrap in plastic and refrigerate overnight.

Grill:

Game Day:

Make the braising liquid by mixing wine, Worcestershire sauce, honey, vinegar, and garlic powder. Heat through and stir.

Lay rings of onions on a sheet of aluminum foil and add garlic. Lay ribs on top of onion and garlic. Crimp foil around ribs loosely, pour ½ cup braising liquid in each packet, grill on low for 3 hours.

Pour braising liquid into a sauce pan and simmer until it reduces by half. Remove the ribs from the foil and place them directly on the grill. Brush the braising liquid on the ribs and grill until desired- Jeanette and crew like it crispy!

Serve it up:

With a glass of wine and your favorite pasta or potato salad.

Crabby Chicken

Blacktop Chef, Norm Pankow
(25 Bears Fans Inc)

Ingredients:

5	lbs boneless chicken breasts
2	bottles lemon pepper marinade
4	packages of imitation crab meat *(ground course in food processor)*
2	large bags shredded cheese *(four cheese blend)*

Prep:

Marinate the chicken for 4 hours.

Grill:

Grill chicken until no longer pink, then dice. Spread chicken over the bottom of a large size aluminum roasting pan. Spread the crab meat over the chicken. Sprinkle generous amounts of cheese over crab. Place pan on grill, uncovered, for 20 minutes or until cheese is melted.

Serve it up:

Serve it as a side or even as a main dish. Dress it up with diced green onions, and spice it up with Frank's RedHot.

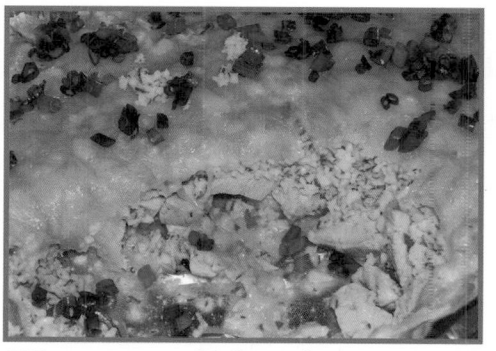

Beer Shrimp

Blacktop Chef, John Moroni

Ingredients:

Jumbo shrimp, beer, basil, minced garlic and olive oil.

Prep and Grill:

Combine ingredients in an aluminum roasting pan. Cook over medium-high heat for ten minutes. Let simmer and keep stirring for 3-5 minutes, or until shrimp is pink. Remove from heat and enjoy!

Rack o' Lamb

Blacktop Chef, John Moroni

Ingredients:

Rack of lamb

Olive oil

Lemon

Garlic, minced

Fresh rosemary

Prep:

1 Day Before

Combine ingredients and rub over both sides of lamb. Marinate overnight.

Grill:

Heat grill to medium-high. Sear lamb on face side and cook for 20 minutes or until done.

Not only can John Moroni cook a great meal, but the man knows a thing or two about presentation. He laid out his lamb on a bed of fresh herbs with a scattering of colorful beer shrimp on the side!

73

ATLANTA FALCONS

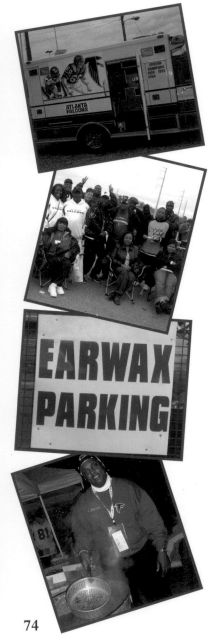

The Bird is Back...

In 2001, Atlanta got a new owner, and a new era in Falcons football was born. When Arthur Blank took over the team, the first thing he did was ask his players what he could do to help make them a winning team.

They told him to pack the stands with screaming fans, so that's what he did.

He started by slashing ticket prices. They sold out the dome, and now have over 36,000 fans on a waiting list for season tickets.

He created interactive game day events, including Falcon's Landing, and leased parking lots around the dome to provide more parking and better tailgating opportunities.

> "Blank understands the game is not just about the players. It's about the people who pay to see them, too. Good for him. Lucky for Atlanta."
>
> -Sportswriter Clark Judge

Blacktop's Best...
Falcon 'Souper' Bowl

Blacktop Chef, Nate Edge

Nate parties at every Falcons' home game with about 25 of his closest fanatic friends. Their Falcon Fan Club makes a 12 hour day of it, cooking up breakfast, lunch, and dinner on the blacktop.

And they know how to party! Their tailgating bar featured one of the coolest contraptions we found -- a rotating shot dispenser that holds 6 bottles of liquor!

"We work all week and tailgate all weekend. Every time, it's like winning the SuperBowl."

Ingredients:

4	chicken breasts
4	carrots, chopped
4	potatoes, chopped
2	onions, chopped
4	tomatoes, chopped
3	cans sweet corn
10	fresh okra, chopped
2	cans lima beans
1	can tomato sauce

Salt and pepper

Prep and Cook:

In a cast iron Dutch oven, salt water and boil chicken until tender.

Remove and debone chicken. Empty Dutch oven and place chicken back in. Cover with water and bring to a boil.

Add remaining ingredients and simmer 30 minutes.

Serve it up:

Serve with cornbread or crackers, and spice it up with some Frank's RedHot!

Easy Game Day Dip

Blacktop Chef, James Martin

Ingredients:

1	lb Jimmy Dean hot or spicy sausage
1	lb Velveeta cheese
12	oz can white corn
12	oz can yellow corn
16	oz salsa *(or try Garpeno!)*

EZ Prep:

Brown crumbled sausage in bottom of small Dutch oven. Turn off heat.

Cube Velveeta and stir into sausage until melted.

Add corn and salsa, stir until well mixed.

Serve it up:

Serve immediately. The Dutch oven will keep the dip warm for awhile. Rewarm as needed over low flame, stirring occasionally to prevent cheese from burning on the bottom.

The Basic Bar

Liquors:
Rum
Whiskey
Gin
Tequila
Vodka
Triple Sec

Liqueurs:
Peach Schnapps
Sour Apple Pucker
Kahlúa
Irish Cream

Mixers:
Sodas
Rose's sweet and sour
OJ
Rose's lime juice
Cranberry
Tonic water
Bloody Mary Mix

Garnish:
Green olives
Lemon & lime wedges
Coarse salt

If You Build It

Nothing draws a bigger crowd of tailgaters than a bad-ass tailgating bar. (Consider therefore, very carefully, just how popular you really want to be before reading on...)

BEER BONG! SHOT! SHOT! SHOT! YEAH... is the sound of a great frat party. OK, maybe some tailgates go that way, but being the best bartender in the lot can be a combination of killer shots and a well stocked bar.

Hi, my name is Jay, and I am a bartender. So, let's get started. Although alcohol can break your bank, don't buy the cheapest thing on the shelf-- unless it's for your ex! A good mid-priced whiskey or bourbon will do. I always recommend Jack Daniel's, but then again, I don't drink much (attempt at sarcasm).

Tip #1: Buy what YOU like to drink.

Mixers are important! Sodas and juices need to be fresh and plentiful.

Tip #2: Buy your juices in small cans, sodas in 12 ounce cans and tonics in small glass bottles. Don't forget to recycle!

Don't forget the garnishes, and prepare them ahead of time. Wedge your lemons and limes the night before the tailgate and put them in a resealable container in the fridge. If you are doing Bloody Marys, have your celery stalks cleaned, cut and ready to go the night before as well.

Tip #3: Minimize your work at the tailgate by doing what you can the day before.

After the last shot is poured and the party's over, you have to store your bar for the next tailgate. Plastic tubs from your local hardware store are a godsend. These babies make storing and transporting your bar easy and convenient.

Tip #4: Make your bar easy to store and move.

Using pour spouts on your bottles is the only way to go. It makes pouring more accurate and less messy.

Tip #5: To reduce alcohol evaporation, replace the bottles original cap when storing. Alcohol waste is a serious offense in most states!

-Jay

Chicken and Sausage Stew

Blacktop Chefs, Jim & Justin Kirk

Jim and Justin tailgated with us and shared Jim's mom's recipe for a hearty, downhome dish sure to "warm the heart on a cold day of tailgating!"

Ingredients:

1	lb sausage, sliced diagonally	2	Tbsp flour
4	boneless skinless chicken breasts, cooked and cubed	1	28 oz can diced tomatoes, drained
6	Tbsp oil	1	tsp dried thyme
3	celery stalks, chopped diagonally	1	tsp red pepper flakes
2	carrots, chopped diagonally	1/2	Tbsp black pepper
2	onions, chopped	1/2	Tbsp salt
1	green bell pepper, chopped	3	14.5 oz cans chicken stock
2	cloves garlic, minced	2	cups long grain white rice, cooked

Prep, Cook, and Serve:

Heat 2 Tbsp oil over med-high heat in large Dutch oven. Add chicken, brown, remove, and set aside.

Add 2 Tbsp oil to sauté onion, celery, carrots, bell pepper and garlic.

Stir in flour. Add tomatoes, pepper flakes, thyme, salt and pepper.

Add stock. Bring to a boil over med-high heat. Add chicken and rice. Lower heat, cover. Simmer until liquid is mostly absorbed. Add sausage.

Serve hot, with a cold beer!

The Basic Bar

continued...

Basic Equipment Essentials

- Ice chest with ice
- Small cutting board & knife
- Shaker & strainer set
- Jigger or shot glass
- Tub with rinse water
- Liquid sanitizer
- 3-4 bar towels
- Plastic cups
- Plastic shot glasses
- Pour spouts
- Drink guide
- Drink menu
- Plastic tub for storage
- Straws
- Toothpicks

An easy way to build a... Bad-Ass Bar

Once you have your basic bar set-up, you need to replenish as you drink. In addition to restocking, try to feature a new drink every tailgate. This new drink should be exotic enough to warrant a trip to the liquor store. By featuring a new drink every tailgate, your bar will soon rival any establishment in town.

Try Toni's Chocolate Cake Shot:

1 1/2	oz SKYY Vodka
1	oz Frangelico

Sugar coated lemon wedges

Mix vodka and Frangelico in shot glass. Bite the lemon and take the shot. You'll see, it tastes like chocolate cake!

Georgia Boll'd P-nuts

Ingredients:

Raw peanuts

Water to cover

Sea salt

Optional seasonings:

  Cajun

  garlic powder

Prep and Cook:

Thoroughly wash raw peanuts in cold water, then soak about 30 minutes. Drain.

Put peanuts in large cast iron Dutch oven, and cover with water.

Add salt, approximately 1 cup for every 1 gallon of water.

Add seasoning, to taste, if desired.

Cover and boil about 4-6 hours, until shells are soft and nuts are the consistency of a canned bean. Some people like them firmer, others mostly mush. You'll have to test and taste until they seem "done" to you.

Serve:

Remove peanuts from water with a large slotted spoon. Serve hot, room temp, or chilled, in shells. Crack open and slurp the nuts and brine from the shell. YUM!

"The Caviar of the South"

During football season, you can hardly drive down the road anywhere in the South without passing by a roadside boiled peanut stand -- or two or three.

Rolling in salty vats beneath a cloud of steam that smells a lot like dirt, this seasonal Southern delicacy is, depending who you ask, either a slimy, mushy abomination or the tender taste of home.

For me, it was neither. While my only Southern blood comes from somewhere south of the Rio Grande, these sinfully salty and strangely addictive snacks are something I'd gladly drive to Georgia for. Good thing I found a recipe that's the next best thing to the authentic "green" variety boiled fresh out of the ground during peanut harvest between August and November.

In Georgia, you can buy boiled peanuts (or boll'd p-nuts as the more rustic signs read) at peanut stands, convenience stores, and even the supermarket. Often they're kept warm in crockpots, before being dished up into styrofoam coffee cups.

Enjoy them warm or cold, according to preference. They can be stored in the fridge for days (if they last that long!) or frozen in zippered baggies and then microwaved when you have a craving.

While Georgia can't lay sole claim to the delight that is the boiled peanut (they're popular throughout the South and enjoyed in Asia as well) they are so much a part of the culture here that local 4-H groups recently collected over $10,000 for Operation Boiled Peanut.

The money was used to send more than two tons of boiled peanuts to Baghdad for the soldiers of Georgia Army National Guard's 48th Brigade Combat Team.

Boiled peanuts are the taste of Georgia that can not be missed.

The perfect tailgate food, you can pass the pre-game hours peeling and slurping and tossing the shells. They're absolute heaven served chilled with a cold beer on a hot day. And later in the season, served fresh out of the pot with a glass of bourbon, they're a treat that will warm you through and through.

Smokin' 101

Here's a basic primer to help clear up some of the smoke... (before you go drop five grand on one of these babies!)

Smoking:

Food cooks slower at a lower temperature; 180-250 degrees.

Dry Smoking:

With indirect heat and a closed lid, vents are used to regulate heat and smoke levels.

Wet Smoking:

Uses a pan of water, beer, juice, or... inside the smoker to create a moist heat and juicier meat.

Woods:

The wood from any fruit-bearing trees work well for smoking, and each infuses your meat with a slightly different flavor. Avoid using a lot of bark, as it can give your meat a bitter taste.

Build a basic smoker:

If you want to give smoking a try, you can build a basic smoker from a barrel drum or a trash can, or even modify your grill to act like a smoker. Search online for plans...

Smokin' hot trailer set-ups!

From New York to Arizona we saw some killer smoker trailers, but nowhere more so than at the Thanksgiving tailgate in Dallas. Surprised? Here, the aroma of smoldering applewood, hickory, and mesquite hung heavy in the air as birds destined for the holiday table warmed slowly toward perfection.

These enormous cylindrical smoke chambers come in many shapes and sizes, and are towed behind trucks and motorhomes like a badge of BBQ honor (and many of them have the blue ribbons to prove it!)

Once the equipment of only professional pitmasters and competitive cooks, smoker trailers are becoming ever-more popular in tailgating lots as men, being men, admire--then acquire-- these works of culinary art.

The basic unit can set you back several thousand, and the bigger, custom jobs go for upwards of ten. So many groups will pool their funds to buy one for the common cause.

And why?

The popular models can cook as much as 100 pounds of meat, and allow you to cook chickens, ribs, pork roasts, salmon and sausages all at the same time!

Many trailers come with a traditional grill, griddle, and/or warming rack for heating up sauces and side dishes.

It takes time, and attention, to keep the temperature steady and the smoke going, but the results are well worth it: moist, tender, and flavorful meat, AND the envy of fellow tailgaters!

DALLAS COWBOYS

Turkey Day, Cowboy Style

When you say "tailgate party" the image that comes to most people's minds is that of a beer guzzlin', brat grillin' testosterone-fest. And in many cases, that's pretty close to accurate.

But in Dallas, on Thanksgiving, it's so much more.

For many fans, it has become a holiday tradition and they come out, year after year, to celebrate with the whole family.

We met a family who'd traveled down from Denver together in a killer custom toter-home.

And another who'd chartered tour busses to haul in the entire extended clan -- all couple hundred of them -- for a Thanksgiving Day family reunion.

We saw aunts and uncles, cousins and grandparents gathering around long, cloth covered tables to share a sit-down dinner of turkey and all the trimmings.

And though we didn't see any turduckens, there was something in the air that made you feel like you were a part of something even bigger!

Blacktop's Best...

Cevapcici with Ajvar

Blacktop Chef, Bart Beaudry

A New York transplant turned diehard Cowboys fan, Bart hauls around a tailgating trailer with a huge Dallas helmet painted on the side. It's filled with the coolest tailgating gear to enjoy with his whole family.

His eclectic menu featured smoked turkey legs (with whole garlic cloves buried in the meat!), ginger shrimp, nachos with fresh salsa, and homemade flan. It was hard to choose a favorite! But this Croatian sausage served with a roasted red pepper sauce was the thing that really won over our judges!

Cevapcici

Ingredients:

1	lb ground beef
1	lb ground pork butt
1	lb ground lamb

use 15% fat for meats, not lean

1	tsp Vegeta Seasoning
1/2	tsp onion powder
1/2	tsp garlic salt
1	egg

Prep and Cook:

Mix meats thoroughly by hand.

Add Vegeta, onion, garlic, and egg. Mix well by hand until spices are evenly distributed throughout. Refrigerate 2 hours, or until firm.

Roll into cigar sized sausages, and grill until done (20 minutes at 300 degrees).

Serve it up:

These are great served on a skewer, with plenty of ajvar for dipping!

Ajvar Sauce

Ingredients:

2	large eggplants
6	large red sweet peppers
1	clove garlic, minced
1	lemon, juiced
1/2	cup olive oil

Salt and pepper

Parsley, minced

Prep and Cook:

Bake eggplants and peppers at 350 degrees until tender when pierced with fork.

Peel skins off hot veggies, then mince. Season to taste.

Add garlic and lemon.

Stir in as much oil as veggies will absorb.

Mix well, and sprinkle parsley on top.

Serve it up:

As a dipping sauce, a condiment for grilled meats, or sandwich spread!

Godzilla Salsa

**Another great recipe from:
The Beaudry Family**

"We can never make enough of this salsa! It's all fresh vegetables, nothing artificial... and the whole family, friends and neighbors LOVE IT!!!"

Ingredients:

5   heads of garlic

1   bunch of cilantro
    (LOTS of it)

1 1/2   purple Bermuda
        onions

4   lbs plum tomatoes
    (no seeds)

juice of 2 limes

juice of 2 lemons

1   habanero pepper

2   jalapeno peppers

Salt and pepper to taste

Prep and Cook:

Finely chop all ingredients, add lemon and lime juices and salt and pepper to taste.

Serve:

This stuff is so great, all you need is a spoon. Serve in a bowl with tortilla chips. Also great over fresh grilled fish!

Smo-Fried Turkey

Blacktop Chef, Omar Cantu

Can't decide if you like your turkey better deep-fried or smoked? Try both! This recipe gives you all the flavor of smoking, plus the juicy meat and crispy golden skin that fried fans love!

Ingredients:

16   lb turkey, fresh or thawed

2   gallons peanut oil

1/4   cup rub *(equal parts)*

      **Cajun seasoning
      kosher salt
      coarse ground pepper**

1/4   cup marinade *(equal parts)*

      **onion juice
      garlic juice
      Crystal Hot Sauce**

Mesquite wood

Prep:

1 Day Before:

Thoroughly clean turkey and pat dry.

Rub seasonings into skin, and inject marinade into meat. Cover and refrigerate overnight.

Smoke:

Game Day:

Smoke turkey for 4 hours at a low temp, somewhere around 180 degrees, according to smoker manufacturer's directions. *Omar likes to use mesquite wood!*

Remove turkey from smoker.

Fry:

Heat peanut oil to 350 degrees in aluminum turkey fryer.

Carefully lower smoked turkey into oil, and fry 30 minutes or until internal temperature reaches 170 degrees.

Remove and let stand 30 minutes before carving.

Serve it up:

This is one spicy bird, but it still goes well with the traditional Thanksgiving fixins. Or team it up with red beans and rice and corn on the cob!

Cowboy Chicken

Blacktop Chef, Michael Alianell

This easy prep and delicious recipe is sure to keep your friends coming around, if you want 'em!

Ingredients:

1	bag of boneless chicken breasts
1	bottle Italian dressing
3	cups BBQ sauce

Prep:

Pour the bottle of Italian dressing in the bag of chicken and marinate overnight.

Grill:

Heat to medium and grill for 14 minutes or until done. Brush BBQ sauce over chicken during the last minute. Slice breasts and brush one more time with light coat of BBQ sauce.

Serve it up:

"Put it on a plate and get the heck out of the way. STAMPEDE!"

"Mimosa?" Of course, with a cool drink tower like this, we had to stop and try one. OK, more than one, but what a cool drink tower! Every tailgater NEEDS one of these babies!

Apple Smoked Pork Butt

Blacktop Chef, Steven Chisolm

Ingredients:

1	30 lb pork butt
1/2	gallon apple cider
1/4	cup red pepper flakes
1/4	cup garlic, minced
2	Tbsp thyme

Prep and Cook:

Place pork in a pan and mop with combined ingredients. Smoke with pecan wood, 2 hours per pound.

Serve it up:

Slice it right off the butt!

This is a BIG recipe for a BIG piece of meat and a BIG smoker to feed a BIG crowd!

TAMPA BAY BUCCANEERS

Aargh! Thar be a Party...

When a football team puts a full-sized pirate ship inside their stadium, there's just something that says to you "We're here to party!"

The warm air pulses with a fun, festive atmosphere as tailgate parties spill down the surrounding streets and vendors sell hand-rolled cigars on the corners.

Football Town USA, an interactive fan experience, and a massive all-inclusive Official Tailgate Party complete with live music provide fans with a chance "to get their Buc on" before gametime!

But the real diehards still haul out the grills, coolers and pop-up canopies for their own pre-game activities -- mainly relaxing on grass medians beneath swaying palm trees while drinking beers and deep-frying turkeys. (This definitely is not *Green* Bay!)

Groups of loyal fans organize massive events in nearby parks that look more like a family picnic than a tailgate party!

And through it all, the cannons boom and smoke rises from inside the stadium into a blue Florida sky.

Blacktop's Best...

Cap'n Willie's Gumbo

Blacktop Chef, Willie Washington

Willie and his crew of pirates laid claim to the best tailgate island in the lot. When it came time for the Taste-off, all of Willie's mates came over to help cheer their captain to victory!

His gumbo was up against one of the best burgers we've seen yet, and a great grilled steak. But when Willie learned that smack-talk was encouraged, he jumped right in. Soon, his whole tailgate crew was whooping as he fired off insults at the competition... with a smile!

Ingredients:

1	box Zatarain's Gumbo Mix *(base mix without rice)*
1	16 oz bag frozen Okra, sliced
1	lb chicken, chopped
1/2	lb beef sausage, sliced
1/2	lb white perch, chopped
1/2	lb scallops, whole
1/2	lb Gulf shrimp, tail-on
3/4	Tbsp cayenne pepper

Salt and pepper to taste

Prep:

The first thing you've got to remember about gumbo is that traditionally the primary ingredients for this dish are left-overs, tossed into a pot together and simmered until... heaven.

Gumbo recipes, therefore, assume the meats you are using are already cooked. If you're starting with fresh ingredients, any method of precooking will do. Pan fry, grill, or boil... it's up to you!

Willie says go ahead and throw it in raw, and simmer it in the broth. You can adjust various quantities, too, as long as it adds up to 3 pounds.

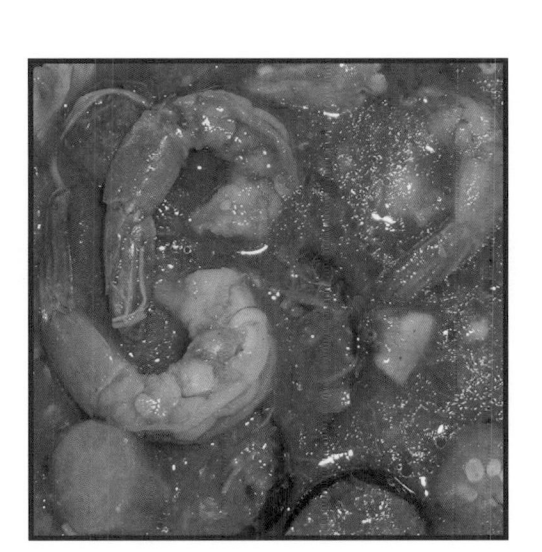

Cook & Serve:

In a cast iron Dutch oven, cook the Zatarain's mix according to directions.

Add okra and cayenne pepper. Simmer for 15 minutes.

Add chicken, sausage, perch and scallops. Simmer for 30 minutes.

Add shrimp, salt and pepper. Simmer for at least 10 minutes more before serving in a bowl over rice.

MGD Steak

Blacktop Chef: Nicholas Silva

When we asked Nicholas what the name of his recipe was, he looked at his beer and said, "MGD Steak!"

Ingredients:

Flank steaks

1	lg onion, sliced
6	limes

Adobo seasoning

Prep:

Cut steaks into 4-5 inch pieces and squeeze fresh lime juice over the top. Shake adobo seasoning over steaks and add sliced onion. Marinate for at least 1 hour.

Grill:

Grill on medium heat until done.

Serve it up:

Serve with tortillas, guacamole, salsa and cheese.

Team Blacktop Tip:

Flank Steaks are a favorite among tailgaters because they cook quickly. But, be careful, over cooking will result in chewy meat!

Drunk'n Loin

Blacktop Chef, The Buc-Bear Boys

These guys cooked up a simple, tasty tailgating treat, but by the time the Taste-off rolled around, they'd eaten it all up. But, not before we got a bite! A taste was all we needed to know that it must go in the book.

Ingredients:

1	4 lb boneless pork loin
1	750 ml bottle of Jim Beam

Lawry's Seasoned Salt

Salt and pepper

Prep:

2-3 Days Before:

Put pork loin in a zipper bag and pour in 1/2 the bottle of Jim Beam, save the other half for the tailgate! Squeeze all the air out of the bag and zip closed. Refrigerate for 2-3 days.

Grill:

Heat grill to medium and fill a drip pan half full of water to keep the loin moist. Rub Lawry's, salt and pepper on loin. Place loin on oiled grill directly over drip pan. Close lid and cook 15 minutes per pound, turning once.

Buccaneer Burger

Blacktop Chef, Tina Simon

"Once you eat these, you'll never go back to regular burgers..."

Ingredients:

2	lbs ground chuck
1	tsp Worcestershire sauce
2	jalapeno peppers, chopped
1	lg onion, chopped
1/2	cup shredded cheddar cheese
1/2	cup shredded jack cheese

Prep:

Mix all ingredients and shape into patties.

Grill:

Grill until done.

Serve it up:

Serve on hamburger rolls with desired condiments.

Garpeno Wraps

Blacktop Chef, Vicki Giallombardo

Vicki introduced us to our first taste of Garpeno. Wow! This stuff rocks! The cool thing is you can use it on, or in, almost anything.

Ingredients:

1	package of tomato basil tortilla wraps
1	jar of Garpeno
32	oz cream cheese

Prep and Serve:

Strain oil from the Garpeno and discard. Put the remaining ingredients in a large mixing bowl. Add cream cheese and mix well.

Spread mixture on wrap and roll the wrap tight. Keep rolling until all the mixture is gone.

Refrigerate for at least 2 hours.

Slice wraps at a diagonal, about an inch thick. Use a toothpick to hold together if necessary.

Smoke 'em if you got 'em!

Around a hundred years ago, Tampa was the Cigar Capital of the World. When Vincente Ybor moved his cigar factory from Key West to avoid labor problems and allow room for expansion, he established Ybor City to house his workers. It attracted cigar makers from across the globe and put Tampa (meaning *sticks of fire*) on the map.

Business boomed, and then dwindled over the years, but a new boom that began in the 1990's has made Ybor hip once again.

Though cigar making is now done on a much smaller scale, as more of a novelty than a necessity, Ybor is home to more than a few cigar shops and bars where you can watch cigars being rolled, stock up your humidor, or smoke one with a good scotch.

Cigars 101

If you've ever walked into a cigar shop and felt overwhelmed by the selection, here are a few tips:

Generally, the darker the wrapper the stronger the flavor. Want something mild? Look for a *Natural* or *Connecticut*. Something more robust? Try a *Maduro*.

Cigars come in various sizes, each with exotic sounding names, and specific length and ring gauge.

For example, *Coronas* are 5 ½ to 6 inches long, with a ring gauge of 42 to 45.

Toros are 6 to 6 ½ inches long, with a ring gauge of 48 to 50.

Shape is categorized as *parejo* or *figurado*. Parejos are uniform and cylindrical. Figurados are more irregularly shaped, often with bulged middles and pointed ends.

CAROLINA PANTHERS

Southern Style...

Somehow, a sense of that old Southern hospitality permeates a Panther tailgate. Maybe it's in the sweet drawl of their words, or their unhurried attitudes, or their readiness to offer you a chair (and a beer) and share their stories.

In this old city that feels so modern and new, fans young and old come out to support their team. There were more women-- and more couples tailgating together-- than anywhere else on the Tour. They come out to the tailgating lots in khakis and golf shirts, and stroll past the white tents and picket fences of the South Lawn Village on their way into the stadium.

It's all very civilized...

And then you meet the guys from the Panthers Huddle. They draw a huge crowd for every home game to a party that's significantly more... frat house. "We like our football with beer, buddies, and babes," they say.

Sounds like a recipe for a great tailgate!

Blacktop's Best...
Bacon-Wrapped Venison

Blacktop Chef, Dal Luke

By the time we met Dal in Carolina, we'd already seen bacon-wrapped venison on the grill at three different stadiums. Just one taste, and we knew why!

Venison, like all game, tends to be much leaner than domestically raised meat. It's easy to overcook, which leads to tough, dry meat. Not so with these melt-in-your-mouth morsels!

See, wrapping the bites in bacon (a method known as *barding*) imparts a moist, fatty flavor the meat wouldn't have on it's own, while sealing in the best of the venison. Great tip!

Ingredients:

Venison steaks

1	bottle Zesty Italian dressing
1	package bacon, unflavored

Lawry's Seasoned Salt

Pepper

Prep:

1 Day Before:

Cut venison into steaks about 1\2 inch thick.

Pound the venison with a meat mallet on each side until very thin and thoroughly tenderized.

Place the meat in a bowl or resealable storage bag and pour in Italian dressing. Marinate overnight.

Game Day:

Cut the bacon in half to reduce the length of the strip. Remove the steak from the marinade and roll the steaks up, much like a cigar. Wrap the 1\2 slice of bacon around the steaks and secure with a toothpick. Some steak pieces may be too large for bite size so you may have to cut them to size. You want the final product to be about two bites worth. Sprinkle the meat with Lawry's and pepper.

Cook:

Place on a medium heat grill and cook to your satisfaction. Try using the "cold" side of the grill for gas grills to prevent the bacon from causing fire flare ups. For charcoal, you can cook directly over the coals. Don't cook too fast!

Tip: try adding a piece of jalapeno or banana pepper rolled up inside of the venison!

Serve it up:

These can be served right off the grill as appetizers or a main dish.

Go Blue!

Our Superfan friend "Carolina Clay" is a whole pep squad rolled into one spirited package! He pulls into the lot in a convertible Cruiser covered in custom Panther Paws and sporting a pop-up tailgate canopy. He wears a homemade suit and spreads his Panther cheer, handing out pom-poms, beads, and stickers to his tailgating neighbors.

The Brews Bros.

Wearing backpacks full of coffee and holsters full of cups, these guys made their way through the lots filling up early tailgaters with complimentary caffeine. We gotta get ourselves one of those!

Carolina Panthers

"The Birthplace of BBQ"

Ask anyone in Carolina and they'll tell you, this is the place where it all started. There may be some debate as to whether it began with the early settlers, African slaves, or even the marauding buccaneers, but one thing is for sure -- around here barbecue has nothing to do with cooking burgers and dogs on the backyard grill.

Barbecue, for one thing, is always pork. And depending on whether it's done in the Western tradition or the Eastern, it's either the pork shoulder or the whole hog.

Slow cooked on a wood fire at around 250 degrees for 16-18 hours, the meat is continuously mopped with a vinegar-based sauce that has little in common with commercial BBQ sauces.

It is meant primarily to keep the meat moist, and to bring out the natural flavor in the pork.

Traditional Tarheel "Sauce"

1 cup white vinegar
1 cup cider vinegar
1 Tbsp brown sugar
1 Tbsp cayenne pepper
1 Tbsp Frank's RedHot Sauce
1 tsp sea salt
1 tsp ground black pepper

Make at least a day before the hog roast for best flavor. Blend well. Store in airtight container in fridge for up to 2 months.

90

Dead Falcon Parmesan

Blacktop Chef, Mel Hyder

Ingredients:

6	boneless chicken breasts
1	jar marinara sauce
1	lg green pepper, sliced
6	lg mushrooms, sliced
2	Tbsp olive oil

Granulated garlic

Kosher salt

Fresh cracked pepper

Italian seasoning

Mozzarella cheese, deli sliced

Prep:

Shake to combine garlic, salt, pepper and Italian seasoning and rub into chicken breasts. Grill until no longer pink in the center.

Cook:

Heat grill to low-medium. Place the chicken in a cast iron skillet and cover with sauce, peppers and mushrooms. Cover and simmer for 15-20 minutes making sure to turn the chicken at least once.

Serve it up:

Traditionally, this dish is served with pasta. But, a good loaf of bread and salad is the perfect fit for a tailgate!

Falcon & Dumplings

Blacktop Chef, Harriett Furr

Ingredients:

1	lg whole chicken
3	cups self-rising flour

Salt and pepper

optional:
carrots, celery, onions & garlic

Prep, Cook & Serve:

Boil chicken with skin in a cast iron Dutch oven until chicken is cooked through and you have a rich broth left over. Remove chicken from broth, debone and set aside.

Sift flour add salt and pepper to taste. Put flour in a large bowl and shape into a volcano. Pour one cup broth plus one half cup water and work with your hands like kneading bread.

Roll out like pie dough and cut into strips, break into one inch pieces and drop into boiling broth. Add chicken and simmer for 15 minutes. Serve.

***Dunk the dumplings. Don't stir, because they WILL fall apart!

Knot Yet Chili

Blacktop Chef, Julie Hines

Ingredients:

4	lbs ground beef
1	green pepper, chopped
1	Vidalia onion, chopped
1	bunch of celery, chopped
4	16 oz cans pinto beans, drained
4	28 oz cans whole tomatoes
1 1/2	cups Merlot
1 1/2	Tbsp oregano
1 1/2	Tbsp cayenne pepper
1	Tbsp chili powder

Prep & Cook:

In a cast iron Dutch oven, brown ground beef and drain. Add onions, green pepper, celery and pinto beans. "Squish" whole tomatoes with hands into Dutch oven. Add wine, then spices. Simmer on low for several hours.

Serve it up:

Serve with cheese and chips or bread.

"Snow, sleet, rain or shine… never miss a home game! I promise my chili will warm your soul. Spoon in one hand, beer in the other! Don't forget the friends!"

"If you use Texas Pete in my chili, I'll be pissed!"
                    -Julie Hines

NEW ORLEANS SAINTS

Food, Friends and FAITH!

There's something to be said for fans who won't even let a hurricane, a flood, and the loss of their stadium dampen their team spirit.

All season long, we'd heard stories from fans across the NFC about the killer tailgates they can always count on whenever the Saints come to town.

Traveling with their massive gumbo tubs and stock pots, they're always sure to cook up a good time, we were told.

The scene in Baton Rouge, at their temporary home at LSU, had been downgraded from a full-blown N'Awlins style bash, but the food and the hospitality lived up to the legend.

And even while some were without homes to live in, they still managed to find themselves at home in their tailgating neighborhood.

Grilling sausages on a crisp December morning, they smiled as the sunlight glinted from the gold letters of their new team motto... FAITH.

Blacktop's Best...
Kickin' Seafood Gumbo

Blacktop Chef, Werner Coston

What can you say about a tailgate crew that has a bouncy castle for the kids?

When Werner and company brought over their signature gumbo to the Taste-off-- they came with attitude and all!

Not surprisingly, Werner's was just one of a handful of gumbos competing in the New Orleans Taste-off. But his cool confidence combined with the smokin' taste of his lot-famous gumbo were a true recipe for success!

Ingredients:

Roux:

1	cup flour
1	cup oil

4	quarts chicken broth
1 1/2	lbs fresh okra, sliced
3	onions, chopped
1	cup green onions, chopped
1	cup celery, chopped
5	cloves garlic, minced
1	lb Gulf shrimp, peeled
1	lb crawfish tails
2	lbs hot smoked sausage, sliced

Salt and pepper

Cayenne pepper

Cook:

Roux:

In a cast iron skillet, combine flour and oil. Cook over medium heat, stirring constantly until color is medium brown to copper. Remove from heat and set aside.

Gumbo:

In a cast iron Dutch oven, brown sausage. Remove sausage and set aside.

Add okra to Dutch oven and sauté in sausage drippings.

Add onion, green onion, garlic and celery. Sauté until transparent.

Add roux and mix well. Stir in chicken broth and sausage. Season with salt, pepper and cayenne to taste.

Simmer for one hour, then add shrimp and crawfish tails. Bring to a boil, then remove from heat. Cover and let stand for at least 30 minutes.

Serve it up:

Serve over rice with Frank's Original RedHot Sauce.

New Orleans Saints

LSU's 'Mike the Tiger' played the perfect host for Team Blacktop and the Saints.

Just call it "good"

Outside Louisiana, there's a bit of confusion between *Cajun* and *Creole* cuisine. The terms are often used interchangeably to describe the foods popular in and around New Orleans. And though they do share some things in common, like gumbo and the Holy Trinity (bell pepper, onion, and celery), they are different in many ways.

Creole cuisine still bears a close resemblance to the French cooking at its roots, utilizing more cream in the sauces and soup bases. It is the flavor of the city of New Orleans, producing such local favorites as beignets and jambalaya.

Think of *Cajun* cooking as *Creole's* countrified cousin. Downhome dishes made with foods that are inexpensive and readily available in the rural areas, *Cajun* recipes are usually family heirlooms honed to perfection through the generations. Crawfish pie, boudin, and dirty rice are popular Cajun fare.

Shrimp 101

Peel 'em:

If the head's still there, pinch it off and throw it away.

Grab the feet and pull around the shrimp. The shell should come off in one piece.

Pinch the tail with one hand, and pull the meat out with the other.

Nobody does it right the first time. Be patient and get some practice in, you'll need it. You'll just have to eat more shrimp to become the expert. What a shame!

Blacktop Boudin

Blacktop Chef, Loyal Saints Fan

Ingredients:

2 1/2	lbs pork butt
1	lb pork liver
2	tsp sea salt
2	tsp fresh ground pepper
2	tsp cayenne
1/2	tsp garlic, minced
1/2	cup green bell peppers, diced
1/2	cup celery, diced
3	bunches green onions, diced
1/2	cup parsley, diced
6	cups cooked rice
1 1/2	inch sausage casings *(about 3-4 feet)*

Prep:

Place pork, liver, salt, pepper, and cayenne in large Dutch oven and cover with water. Simmer until meat falls apart. Remove meat, reserve broth.

In a food processor, grind meat, liver, garlic, peppers, celery, onions, and parsley (hold out 1/2 cup parsley and onions).

Gradually stir remaining parsley, onions and rice into mixture, along with enough broth to moisten thoroughly. Use a sausage stuffer or funnel to fill casings. Refrigerate or freeze until ready to cook.

Grill:

These Saints fans skewered their sausages on bamboo. Cook on low-medium heat until they are warm and the skin is crispy. C'est Bon!

Serve it up:

Enjoy right off the skewer!

Rock & Tee's Bayou Boil

Blacktop Chefs,
Chuck and Joy Osborn

"In loving memory of Rock and Tee."

Ingredients:

3-5	gallons water
20	lbs live crawfish *(or shrimp)*
2	lemons, cut in half
2	oranges, cut in half
6	heads of garlic, cut in half
6	ears of corn, cut in half
5	lbs sausage, cut in 1" pieces
10-12	red potatoes, cut in half
6	med onions, cut in half
12	eggs
1	26 oz box salt
1	4 oz bottle Zatarain's Liquid Crab Boil
4	3 oz boxes Zatarain's Dry Crab Boil
1	bag of ice *(for shrimp)*

Note: Figure 2-3 lbs food per person.

If you are lucky enough to have someone like Rock catch and ship mudbugs fresh from the Bayou, then toss 'em in the pot and prepare to suck some heads! If not, fresh Gulf shrimp with shell on will do just fine.

Prep, Cook and Serve:

In a 34 quart or larger boiling pot with strainer basket, bring water, salt, Zatarain's (Liquid & Dry) to a boil. Leave room in pot for displacement.

Add oranges, lemons, onions, and potatoes (cook 5-10 min).

Add eggs, corn, garlic, and sausage (cook 10-15 min).

Strain ingredients and dump on a table covered with newspaper.

Bring liquid back to a boil.

Add crawfish for 3-5 minutes (or until they turn bright orange).

OR

Add shrimp for 2-3 minutes (or until they turn pink and skin clears away from shrimp)

Stop boiling, add ice and let sit for 10 minutes. Strain and dump the seafood on the same newspaper covered table.

This is a great way to accommodate guests with shellfish allergies!

Crawfish 101

Clean 'em:

About an hour before you start cooking, set up your boiling pot and strainer somewhere you can dump dirty water. Fill your pot with water, and fill your strainer with crawfish. Dunk the strainer full of crawfish several times until they are clean.

You will have to change the water a couple times, so make sure you have a good clean water supply.

Do not leave the crawfish submerged, they need air to stay alive!

Throw away the dead ones and keep your clean ones in a clean ice chest until they are ready to cook.

Peel 'em and Eat 'em:

Twist the head off and set aside.

Peel away a couple layers of shell until you can pinch the meat. Pinching the tail and meat, pull meat out of shell and eat.

Pick up the heads and suck some juice... or not!

95

ARIZONA CARDINALS

Visions of Sugarplums...

'Twas the last tailgate for their last game ever at ASU, and Cardinals fans were as anxious as a kid on Christmas Eve.

Maybe that's because it *was* Christmas Eve, and they knew that this year Santa was bringing them a brand new stadium of their very own!

Complete with a retractable roof and roll-out natural grass playing field (the first on their block, and all of North America, for that matter) they couldn't wait to see their Cardinals play there.

Word is there should be plenty of parking at their new home, about 30 miles away in Glendale, and tailgating will be encouraged.

They've also put in the 120 acre Sportsman's Park, with a Great Lawn and hundreds of shade trees, offering tailgaters a place to escape the sometimes "bake you alive" heat on the blacktop in Arizona.

Think they'll allow the hot tubs in there?

Blacktop's Best...
Beer Butt Chicken

Blacktop Chef, Lawrence Hughes

Christmas came early for Lawrence, when Santa's elves (in the guise of tailgating Cardinal hotties) awarded a new Explorer Grill and BBQ box to him and his tailgating crew.

After seven years of tailgating before all the Cardinals home games in the same location outside Sun Devil Stadium, Lawrence, Brent, Scott, and the rest of the gang will kick-off next year in a new spot at the new stadium with a new grill. And we're sure they'll be cooking up something new!

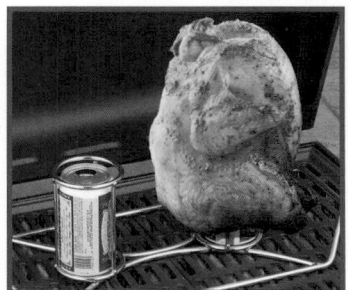

Ingredients:

| 2 | 3 1/2 lb whole chickens |
| 2 | 12 oz cans beer |

Rub:

1	Tbsp oregano
1	Tbsp chili powder
1	Tbsp garlic powder
1	Tbsp brown sugar
1	Tbsp parsley flakes
1	Tbsp cayenne pepper
1	Tbsp pepper

Prep:

Completely thaw your chickens. This is important. A partial thaw will slow cooking time and interfere with consistency.

Trim excess fat from around the cavity opening of the chicken and remove the tail with kitchen shears.

Remove giblets from inside and open a hole under the neck into the cavity. This will allow a vent for the moisture from the can.

Rinse your chickens and pat dry with paper towel. Thoroughly season with rub.

Cook:

Open cans of beer and place them in the can holders.

Place the chickens over the cans.

Cook chickens at 325 for 1-1/2 hours or until chickens are done.

Serve it up:

Just cut and serve as is, or try it in a wrap!

The Twiins...

Beer can chicken has come a long way. The Twiins from Camp Chef will do 2 chickens at the same time on a standard grill.

Sonoran Salsa

Blacktop Chef: Andrea Cordova

Simple, yet tastes sooo good!

Ingredients:

10	jalapenos, diced small
5	tomatoes, diced small
1/2	onion, diced small
2	avocados, diced small
2	limes, juice only
2	tsp salt

Prep:

Combine all ingredients together and mix well. Refrigerate overnight.

Serve:

Serve chilled with tortilla chips. Great with carne asada.

Team Blacktop Tip:

Try adding 4 ounces of your favorite tequila or beer.

Fred Winston's Chili

Blacktop Chef, Cal Kalvzny

Ingredients:

2	lbs ground round
1	lg onion, chopped
1	green bell pepper, chopped
2	jalapeño peppers, chopped
2	cloves garlic, minced
2	Tbsp chili powder
1	Tbsp paprika
1	tsp cumin
1	tsp oregano
1	tsp brown sugar
1	lg can tomatoes, drained
1	can tomato sauce
1	can black beans
1	can red beans
1	can beef broth
1-2	cans flat beer

Prep and Cook:

Brown meat in cast iron Dutch oven. Add onion, peppers, and garlic. Sauté. Stir in seasonings, tomatoes, sauce and beans. Add broth. Cover and simmer 1 hour. Add 1 beer. Simmer uncovered another hour (add more beer as needed).

Serve it up:

Add Frank's Original RedHot Sauce to spice things up.

Cal was cooking up a pot of the legendary chili from Chicago radio icon Fred Winston. When we asked him why he was following Fred's recipe he said, "because everyone knows this is the best chili ever!"

Ass-on-Fire Beans

Blacktop Chef, Tina Sassaman

"This recipe makes an outstanding sweet, tangy dish. It's even better the next day, but by then you'll know why it's called Ass-on-Fire Beans."

Ingredients:

3	lb ground beef
3	onions, finely chopped
1 1/2	tsp garlic powder
3/4	tsp cayenne pepper
1 1/2	tsp oregano
1 1/2	tsp salt
3	8 oz cans tomato sauce
3	32 oz bottles ketchup
1 1/2	lb brown sugar
3	tsp liquid smoke
3	Tbsp chili powder
6	30 oz cans red beans, rinsed

Cook:

In a cast iron Dutch oven, sauté the first six ingredients until the meat is brown and the onion is tender. (Remove most of the grease, but leave some for flavor!)

Add remaining ingredients and stir well to blend. Simmer on low at least one hour. The more it cooks, the more the flavors blend and come out.

Serve it up:

Dish up into bowls, and enjoy with some good bread slathered in real butter.

***Tina says any canned beans will do, kidney, black, Great Northerns, or even a combination.*

Mexican Cornbread

*Blacktop Chef:
Loyal Cardinal Fan*

Ingredients:

1	package cornbread mix
1	egg
2/3	cup milk
1	can cream corn
1	tube Jimmy Dean sausage, cooked, drained and chopped
1	8 oz package 4 cheese mix, shredded

Prep:

Mix all ingredients together in a bowl until moistened.

Cook:

Lightly grease a cast iron Dutch oven or skillet. Heat grill to low. Add mixture and cover for 10-15 minutes. Cornbread is done when a toothpick can be cleanly pulled from the center.

Appendix

Tailgater's Guide to Food Safety...

Nothing ruins a great tailgate party faster than a case of food poisoning! Here's a guide, based on the USDA's *Cooking for Groups*, to help you Play it Safe...

4 Steps to Fight Food Bacteria:

Clean: Wash your hands and your surfaces. Have plenty of water available. Use waterless hand sanitizers and disposable food prep gloves.

Separate: Avoid cross contamination by using separate cutting boards, coolers, mixing bowls and knives for meats and veggies. Prepping and bagging at home can help!

Cook: *Always* use a meat thermometer to check internal temperatures of meat before serving.

Chill: Don't leave food sitting out all day. Serve it, eat it, then cool it!

Plan it Safe:

Make sure you have all the equipment and supplies you'll need to prepare, cook, serve and store *all* your food. Running out of propane can lead to undercooked meat. Run out of ice, you might as well throw it all away. Keep a stock of gloves, antibacterial wipes, hand sanitizer, and plenty of resealable plastic bags in your tailgating gear.

Buy it Safe:

Never buy dented, bulging, or opened items. Check sell-by dates. Frozen foods should be entirely frozen. If they seem like they've started to thaw, don't buy them! Keep meats and veggies separate in you car, your shopping bags, and your cooler. Buy your cold foods last, and take them straight home or transport them in a cooler. Don't drive around with them in your trunk while you run other errands!

Store it Safe:

Store refrigerated items below 40 degrees and frozen items below 0 degrees until ready to thaw and cook. Refrigerate prepared or leftover food within 2 hours. Keep raw meats inside sealed containers so the juices don't drip out and contaminate your other food. Use a separate cooler for your beer and sodas. The constant opening and reopening to get drinks can make it hard to keep your cooler COLD!

Prepare it Safe:

Thaw foods in the fridge, cooler, or in COLD water, then cook immediately Marinate meats in the fridge or cooler, never on the counter. Never reuse marinades, breadings, or batters for other foods. Thoroughly wash all your fresh fruits and veggies in clean water. Only "taste" thoroughly cooked foods with a clean utensil.

Serve it Safe:

Keep cold foods cold. Use trays filled with ice to keep items on your serving table at or below 40 degrees. Keep hot foods hot. Serve straight from the grill, or transfer to chafing dishes, warming trays, or slow cookers. Use a food thermometer to monitor internal temperature, and wash thoroughly between uses. Avoid holding food within the "Danger Zone" between 40 and 140 degrees for longer than 2 hours.

*All temperatures are Fahrenheit. Based on information provided by the United States Department of Agriculture's Food Safety and Inspection Service and the Partnership for Food Safety Education. For more information and to request free copies of their publications, visit them online:

www.fsis.usda.gov
www.fightbac.org.

Weights & Measurements

Abbreviations

oz	ounce(s)
lb(s)	pound(s)
tsp(s)	teaspoon(s)
Tbsp(s)	tablespoon(s)
qt(s)	quart(s)
gal(s)	gallon(s)
grnd	ground
sm	small
med	medium
lg	large

Dry Measure

Pinch	a little less than 1/4 tsp
3 tsp	1 Tbsp
2 Tbsp	1 oz or 1/8 cup
4 Tbsp	2 oz or 1/4 cup
5 1/3 Tbsp	2.7 oz or 1/3 cup
8 Tbsp	4 oz or 1/2 cup
10 2/3 Tbsp	5.4 oz or 2/3 cup
12 Tbsp	6 oz or 3/4 cup
16 Tbsp	8 oz or 1 cup
4 cups	1 qt
4 qts	1 gal

Liquid Measure

3 tsp	1 Tbsp
a dash	a few drops
2 Tbsp	1 oz
4 Tbsp	2 oz or 1/4 cup
5 1/3 Tbsp	2.7 oz or 1/3 cup
8 Tbsp	4 oz or 1/2 cup
10 2/3 Tbsp	6 oz or 3/4 cup
16 Tbsp	8 oz or 1 cup
2 cups	1 pint or 1/2 qt
4 cups	2 pints or 1 qt
4 qts	128 oz or 16 cups or 1 gal

Can Size Equivalents

6 oz	3/4 cup
8 oz	1 cup
10 1/2 oz (No. 1)	1 1/4 cups
15 1/2 oz (No. 300)	1 3/4 cups
16 oz (No. 303)	2 cups
24 oz (No. 2)	2 1/2 cups
46 oz	5 3/4 cups

Herbs & Spices

1 ounce of weight to measurement

Allspice, grnd	5 1/2 Tbsp
Basil	1/2 cup
Bay leaf, whole	7 Tbsp
Black pepper, grnd	1/2 cup
Celery seed	1/4 cup
Cinnamon	5 1/2 Tbsp
Cloves, grnd	5 1/2 Tbsp
Chili powder	1/2 cup + 1 1/2 tsp
Cumin seed	6 Tbsp
Curry powder	5 1/2 Tbsp
Dill weed	6 Tbsp
Dill seed	4 1/2 Tbsp
Garlic powder	6 1/3 Tbsp
Ginger	6 Tbsp
Marjoram	1/2 cup
Mustard, dry grnd	6 Tbsp & 1 tsp
Nutmeg, grnd	5 Tbsp
Onion powder	4 1/2 Tbsp
Oregano	6 Tbsp
Paprika	5 Tbsp
Parsley flakes	1/2 cup + 1 1/2 tsp
Red pepper flakes	1/2 cup + 1 1/2 tsp
Poppy seeds	3 3/4 Tbsp
Rosemary	1/2 cup
Sage	1/2 cup + 1 1/2 Tbsp
Savory	6 3/4 Tbsp
Sesame seed	5 Tbsp
Tarragon	6 3/4 Tbsp
Thyme	6 1/3 Tbsp
Turmeric	5 Tbsp

Weights & Measurements

Butter & Shortening

1 Tbsp	1/2 oz or 1/8 stick
8 Tbsp	4 oz or 1/2 cup or 1 stick
16 Tbsp	8 oz or 1 cup or 2 sticks
3 lb shortening	6 cups
8 oz oil	1 cup

Dairy Products

Eggs

2 raw	1/2 cup

Shredded & Cubed Cheese

4 oz	1 cup cubed or shredded
16 oz	4 cups cubed or shredded

Whipping Cream

1 cup or 8 oz	2 cups whipped

Parmesan or Romano, grated

6 oz	1 cup
16 oz	2 2/3 cups
24 oz	3 cups

Cottage Cheese

6 oz	1 cup
16 oz	2 2/3 cups

Sour Cream

9 oz	1 cup
16 oz	1 3/4 cups

Cream Cheese

3 oz	6 Tbsp or 1/3 cup
8 oz	1 cup
1 lb	2 cups

Condensed Milk

14 oz	1 1/4 cups

Evaporated Milk

6 oz	2/3 cup
14 1/2 oz can	1 2/3 cups
1 cup	3 cups whipped

Dry Milk Powder

16 oz	4 cups dry or 4-5 qts liquid

Buttermilk Powder

12 oz	3 3/4 qts liquid milk
1/4 cup	1 cup milk

Meats

Bacon

8 slices	1/2 cup cooked & crumbled
16 oz	about 18 slices

Beef

1 lb grnd	2 1/2 cups browned
10 lbs grnd	25 cups browned
1 lb raw	3 1/2 cups sliced 3 cups cubed

Bulk Sausage

1 lb raw	2 1/2 cups cooked & crumbled

Chicken:
boneless, skinless

7 1/2 lbs raw	about 25 pieces
1 lb raw	2 cups raw, ground 2 2/3 cups raw, diced
5 lbs raw	12 cups cooked, diced
1 lg breast	3/4 cup cooked, diced
2 1/2 lbs	7-8 lg pieces

Chicken Thighs

5 lbs	about 25 pieces

Whole Chicken

2 1/2 lbs	2 1/2 cups cooked meat
3 1/2-4 lbs	4 cups cooked meat
4 1/2-5 lbs	6 cups cooked meat

Crab Meat:
real or imitation

1 lb cooked & boned	2 cups

Ham

1 lb whole	2 1/2 cups grnd
1 lb whole	3 cups cubed

Turkey Breast

5 lb raw	10 cups cooked meat

Whole Turkey

1 lb	1 cup cooked meat

Tuna Fish

6 oz	3/4 cup lightly packed

YourTailgateParty.com

Fruits & Vegetables

Apples

1 med	1 chopped
1 lb	3 med

Strawberries & Raspberries

4 oz	1 cup
1 pint	1 3/4 cups

Blueberries

1 lb	3 cups

Applesauce

16 oz	2 cups

Bananas

1 lb	3 med or 2 1/2 cups diced or 3 cups sliced
1 med	1/3 cup mashed

Lemons

1 med	3 Tbsp juice & 3 Tbsp grated rind
5-8 med	1 cup fresh juice

Oranges

1	1/3 cup fresh juice

Carrots

1 lb	3 cups sliced or 2 cups diced or 6-8 med
1 med	1/2 cup grated

Onions

1 lb	3 med or 3 cups sliced or 3 cups diced
1 med	1 cup chopped or 1 Tbsp dried, minced or 1 tsp powdered or 2/3 cup sauteed

Green Onions

7 med	1/2 cup sliced

Celery

1 med bunch	4-5 cups diced or 2 1/2-3 cups sauteed or 3 1/2 cups sliced
3 lg ribs	1 1/2 cups diced
1 cup diced	2/3 cup sauteed

Potatoes

1 lb	3 med or 2 3/4 cups diced or 3 cups sliced or 2 cups mashed
5 lbs	10 cups diced or 10 cups mashed

YourTailgateParty.com

Vegetables, Beans & Grains

Spinach & Greens

1 lb raw	10-12 cups torn or 1 cup cooked
10 oz frozen	1 1/2 lbs fresh or 1 1/2 cups cooked

Bell Peppers

1 med	1/2 cup finely chopped
1 lb	5 med or 3 1/2 cups diced

Tomatoes

1 lb	4 small or 1 1/2 cups diced

Cabbage

1 lb	4-5 cups shredded

Garlic

1 med clove	1/8 tsp garlic powder or 1/2 tsp minced

Mushrooms

4 oz fresh	1 cup whole or 1/2 cup cooked
1 lb	4 cups whole or 2 cups cooked or 20 lg or 40 med

Beans

11 oz dry	1 cup dry or 3 cups cooked
15 oz can	1 3/4 cups cooked
16 oz dry	5 cups cooked

Barley

3/4 cup pearl	3/4 cup cooked
1 cup quick	2 1/2 cups cooked

Long Grain White Rice

16 oz dry	2 1/2 cups dry or 10 cups cooked
1 cup dry	7 oz dry or 3 cups cooked

Quick Cooking Rice

1 cup dry	2 cups cooked
12 oz box	5 1/3 cup cooked or 4 1/2 cups half cooked

White Converted Rice

1 cup dry	4 cups cooked

Dry Goods & Miscellaneous

Bread Crumbs

4 slices	2 cups fresh, soft crumbs or 3/4 cup dry crumbs
6 oz dried	1 scant cup

Cereal Crumbs

2 cups flakes	3/4 cup crumbs
21 oz box	7 cups cereal
15 oz puffed rice	11 cups

Flour & Meal

1 lb flour	3 1/2 cups or 4 cups sifted
1 cup	4 oz
14 oz cracker meal	3 3/4 cups

Jams & Jellies

6 oz	2/3 cup
10 oz	1 cup

Cocoa Powder

8 oz	2 cups
16 oz	4 cups

Chocolate Chips

6 oz	1 cup

Ketchup

28 oz	2 1/2 cups

Dressing, Mayo, etc.

1 qt	32 oz or 4 cups

Nuts

2 oz	1/2 cup
16 oz	4 cups

Shredded Coconut

14 oz	3 1/4 cups
16 oz	5 cups

Peanut Butter

16 oz	1 3/4 cups

Ice Cubes

11 cubes	1 cup liquid

Frozen Vegetables

1 oz	3 Tbsp, cooked
4 oz	3/4 cup, cooked
5 oz	1 cup, cooked
10 oz	2 cups, cooked
16 oz	2 3/4 cups, cooked
20 oz	4 cups, cooked

Cooking Temperatures

Times are approximate. Always use a meat thermometer. Temperatures are in degrees Fahrenheit. Temperatures shown are for internal measurement with a meat thermometer.

Beef

Steaks

3/4" thick

3 to 4 min/side   for med rare 145
4 to 5 min/side   for med 160

Kebobs

1 inch cubes

3 to 4 min/side for med rare 145-160

Hamburger Patties

1/2 inch thick

3 min/side for med 160

Roast or Sirloin Tip

3 1/2 to 4 lbs (indirect heat)

20 to 25 min/lb 145-160

4 to 6 lbs (indirect heat)

18 to 22 min/lb 145-160

Ribs or Back

10 min/side for med 160

Tenderloin

2 to 3 lbs

10 to 12 min/side for med rare 145

4 to 6 lbs

12 to 15 min/side for med 160

Ham

Fully cooked (indirect heat)

8 to 10 min/lb 140

Cook-before-eating (indirect theat)

Whole, 10 to 14 lbs

10 to 15 min/lb 160

Half, 5 to 7 lbs

12 to 18 min/lb 160

Portion, 3 to 4 lbs

30 to 35 min/lb

Lamb Chops, Shoulder, Loin or Rib (Rack of)

1 inch thick

5 min/side 145-160

Pork, fresh

Chops

3/4 inch thick

3 to 4 min/side for med 160

1 1/2 inch thick

7 to 8 min/side for med 160

Cooking Temperatures

Times are approximate. Always use a meat thermometer. Temperatures are in degrees Fahrenheit. Temperatures shown are for internal measurement with a meat thermometer.

Pork, fresh

Tenderloin

1/2 to 1 1/2 lbs

15 to 25 min total for med 160

Ribs (indirect heat)

2 to 4 lbs

1 1/2 to 2 hours 160

Venison

Roast, Saddle or Leg

6 to 7 lbs

25 to 30 min/lb 145-160

Steaks or Kebobs, 3/4 inch thick

4 to 5 min/side for med rare 145

6 to 7 min/side for med 160

Chicken

Whole (indirect heat), not stuffed

3 to 4 lbs

60 to 75 min 180 in thigh

5 to 7 lbs

18 to 25 min/lb 180 in thigh

Breast halves

6 to 8 oz each

15 to 15 min/side 170

4 oz each

6 to 8 min/side

Other Parts (legs, thighs, drumsticks, wings and wingettes)

4 to 8 oz

10 to 15 min/side 180

2 to 3 oz

8 to 12 min/side 180

Turkey

Whole (indirect heat), not stuffed

8 to 12 lbs

2 to 3 hours 180 in thigh

12 to 16 lbs

3 to 4 hours 180 in thigh

Other Parts (legs, thighs and drumsticks) Indirect heat

8 to 16 oz

1 1/2 to 2 hours 180

Turkey Roll

2 to 5 lbs

1 1/2 to 2 hours 170-175

5 to 10 lbs

2 to 3 1/2 hours 170-175

Get the Goods!

Brand Names

Get the Goods!

Here you'll find all the brand names used throughout this cook book, where to find them, and maybe some useful information about each one. Grill on... Team Blacktop.

Frank's RedHot Sauce: Cayenne pepper sauce credited with being the secret ingredient in the original Buffalo wing sauce. It's available nationwide in a variety of heats and flavors, including Original, Buffalo Wing, Xtra Hot, and our favorite... Chile n' Lime! *Get it at: www.Franksredhot.com.*

Lawry's Seasoned Salt: Blend of salt, herbs and spices used on the legendary prime rib at Lawry's in Beverly Hills in the 1930's. *Available in grocery stores nationwide.*

Old Bay Seasoning: The all time classic Maryland spice. Use on seafood, poultry, salads, meats and more. Makes delicious steamed crabs and steamed shrimp. Try it on french fries with vinegar! *Get it at: www.marylanddelivered.com/oldbay.*

Bush's Baked Beans: Dog or no dog, these beans speak for themselves. *Available in stores nationwide, or Get it at: www.BushBeans.com.*

Van Camp's Baked Beans: Comes in a variety of flavors, including Honey & Ham. *Available in grocery stores nationwide.*

Maull's: Maull's Genuine Barbecue Sauce was first created in St. Louis, Missouri over 70 years ago from Louis Maull's original family recipe. It is still made exactly the same way today, by the Maull family. *Get it at: www.Maull.com.*

Tecate: Good Mexican beer. *Available in grocery stores nationwide.*

MGD: Good American beer (Miller Genuine Draft, Miller Brewing Company, Milwaukee, WI). *Available in grocery stores nationwide.*

Heinz 57: Heinz often markets the sauce as "ketchup with a kick" to highlight its distinction. *Available in grocery stores nationwide.*

Corona: Another good Mexican beer. *Available in grocery stores nationwide.*

La Pina: The proper name for this flour is 'La Pina Harina De Trigo.' *We don't know where it's available. You'll have to check with your local grocer.*

Brand Names

Mrs. Dash: An all-purpose, versatile blend of 14 savory herbs and spices. *Available in grocery stores nationwide or get it at www.mrsdash.com.*

Emeril's Essence: "My original Essence is perfectly balanced, a blend of spices and herbs to complement meat or fowl, fish, veggies and pasta. I use it on everything but ice cream." *Available in grocery stores nationwide.*

Zatarain's: Zatarain's has been an important part of New Orleans-style cooking for over 100 years and a key ingredient in the city's rich cultural heritage. Zatarain's comes in a variety of different seasonings and recipe flavors. *Available in grocery stores nationwide or get it at www.zatarain.com.*

Yuengling: In addition to the traditional lager, America's Oldest Brewery has a portfolio of six other beers. *Unfortunately, available in limited markets.*

Cuervo 1800: Good Mexican Tequila. *Available nationwide.*

Rose's Lime and Sweet n Sour: made by the British L. Rose & Co., and distributed by Mott's in the US. Rose's is your standard Lime and Sweet n Sour mix in America. *Available in grocery stores nationwide.*

Cointreau: Orange flavored liqueur. *Available nationwide.*

McCormick's Grill Mates: Comes in a variety of flavors of spice blends, marinades and sauces. *Available in grocery stores nationwide.*

Moore's Marinade: Moore's Original Marinade was introduced thirty years ago at a steakhouse in a small town called Jasper, Alabama (just north of Birmingham). *Get it at: www.mooresmarinade.com.*

Goya Mojo: Zesty Mojo Criollo with garlic, onion, and citrus for tender, tasty meat and poultry and Mojo Chipotle for a fiery, smoky flavor. Also try Bitter Orange, perfect on chicken or pork. *Available in grocery stores nationwide or get it at www.goya.com.*

Gulden's Mustard: Charles Gulden established his mustard company in 1862 near the South Street Seaport in New York City. Traditional Gulden's is a spicy brown deli mustard. *Available in grocery stores nationwide.*

Taylor Pork Roll: This is native to the Philly area. The closest substitute would be a Canadian bacon. *Get it at: www.jerseyporkroll.com.*

Lipton's Beefy Onion Soup Mix: This comes in a box with multiple packets. Lipton's has numerous flavors of soup mix. *Available in grocery stores nationwide.*

Brand Names

A.1. Steak Sauce: For 140 years, A.1. has been the perfect complement to steak... from start to finish. Use it as a marinade, brush it on while grilling or just pour it on at the table. *Available in grocery stores nationwide.*

Windsor & Sun-Drop: Windsor is a Canadian whiskey *(available nationwide)* and Sun-Drop is a citrus soda. Goes real good with 'coon huntin' and ice. *Available in stores throughout the Midwest, or get in online at www.sundrop.net.*

XXX Horseradish: The proper name is Royal Bohemian XXX Hot Horseradish Mustard (Brown). Be careful, it's hot. *Get it at: www.wisconline.com/store*

Jimmy Dean Hot n Spicy Sausage: Need we say more. A reliable brand of sausage founded by the country music legend. *Available nationwide.*

Velveeta Cheese: Velveeta is a brand of processed cheese first made in 1918. *Available in grocery stores nationwide.*

Kahlúa: Coffee flavored liqueur from Mexico. *Available nationwide.*

SKYY Vodka: Good vodka in a pretty blue bottle. *Available nationwide.*

Jack Daniel's: Since 1863, Jack Daniel has made his famous Whiskey. Charcoal mellowing is what makes Jack Daniel's a smooth sippin' Tennessee Whiskey. *Available nationwide.*

Jim Beam: Jim Beam is a brand of bourbon whiskey distilled in Kentucky. Founded by Jacob Beam in 1795. *Available nationwide.*

Vegeta: Vegeta is a gourmet seasoning and soup mix from Croatia. *Get it at: www.podravka.com.*

Crystal: THE cayenne pepper sauce of New Orleans, their factory was destroyed by hurricane Katrina. They've relocated, and are resuming production in summer 2006. *Get it at: www.baumerfoods.com*

Texas Pete: Relatively mild brand of tabasco pepper sauce, manufactured in North Carolina and popular throughout the Southeast. *Get it at: www.texaspete.com*

Garpeno: This Giallombardo family recipe is a unique blend of fresh herbs. This stuff will knock your socks off. *Get it at: www.garpeno.com or www.papadominicks.com.*

Tour Hosts

Our Tour Hosts...

Camping.com made sure that we had a place to stop and relax every night. It was much needed after those long driving days on the road.

Everywhere we stayed, we met the greatest people and were welcomed like returning friends.

Team Blacktop wishes to extend a hearty thank you for the hospitality. We look forward to seeing you all again on our next visit.

If you're looking for a great campground or RV park, you'll find these and all the best online at Camping.com!

Bakersfield Palms RV Park, CA

Olema Ranch Campground, CA

RV Park of Portland, OR

Olympia Campground, WA

Spokane KOA, WA

Grandview Campground, MT

Lazy J RV Park, SD

Kiesler's RV Resort, MN

Shipshewana Campground, IN

Countryside Campground, OH

Chestnut Ridge Park, WV

Cherry Hill Park, MD

Drummer Boy Camping Resort, PA

Cross Creek Camping Resort, OH

Sundermeir RV Park, MO

Woodside Lake Park, OH

Indian Creek Camp Campground, MI

Cold Creek Trout Camp, OH

Sleepy Hollow Lake Campground, NY

Buttonwood Campground, PA

81/80 RV Park and Campground, PA

Timberlane Campground, NJ

Normandy Farms, MA

Liberty Harbor RV Park, NJ

Shangri-La on the Creek, PA

Woodside Lake Park, OH

Sky High Camping Resort, WI

Pine Grove Campground, WI

Wisconsin State Fairgrounds, WI

South Bend East KOA , IN

Paradise RV Park, IL

River Road RV and Horsecamp, TN

Springridge RV Park, MS

All Seasons RV Park, TX

Shallow Creek Golf & RV Resort, TX

Gulf Pines KOA, FL

Hide-a-way RV Resort, FL

Flamingo Lake RV Resort, FL

Oak Plantation, SC

River Creek Campground, NC

Orange Blossom RV Park, FL

Isla Oro, FL

Boyd's Campground, FL

Sun n' Fun, FL

Camping on the Gulf, FL

Baton Rouge KOA, LA

Brauning Lake RV Resort, TX

Carslbad RV Park, NM

Good Life RV Park, AZ

Index

Index

Recipe Title:

Ingredients:

Prep:

Cook / Grill:

Serve it up:

Ingredients:

Prep:

Recipe Title:

Cook / Grill:

Serve it up:

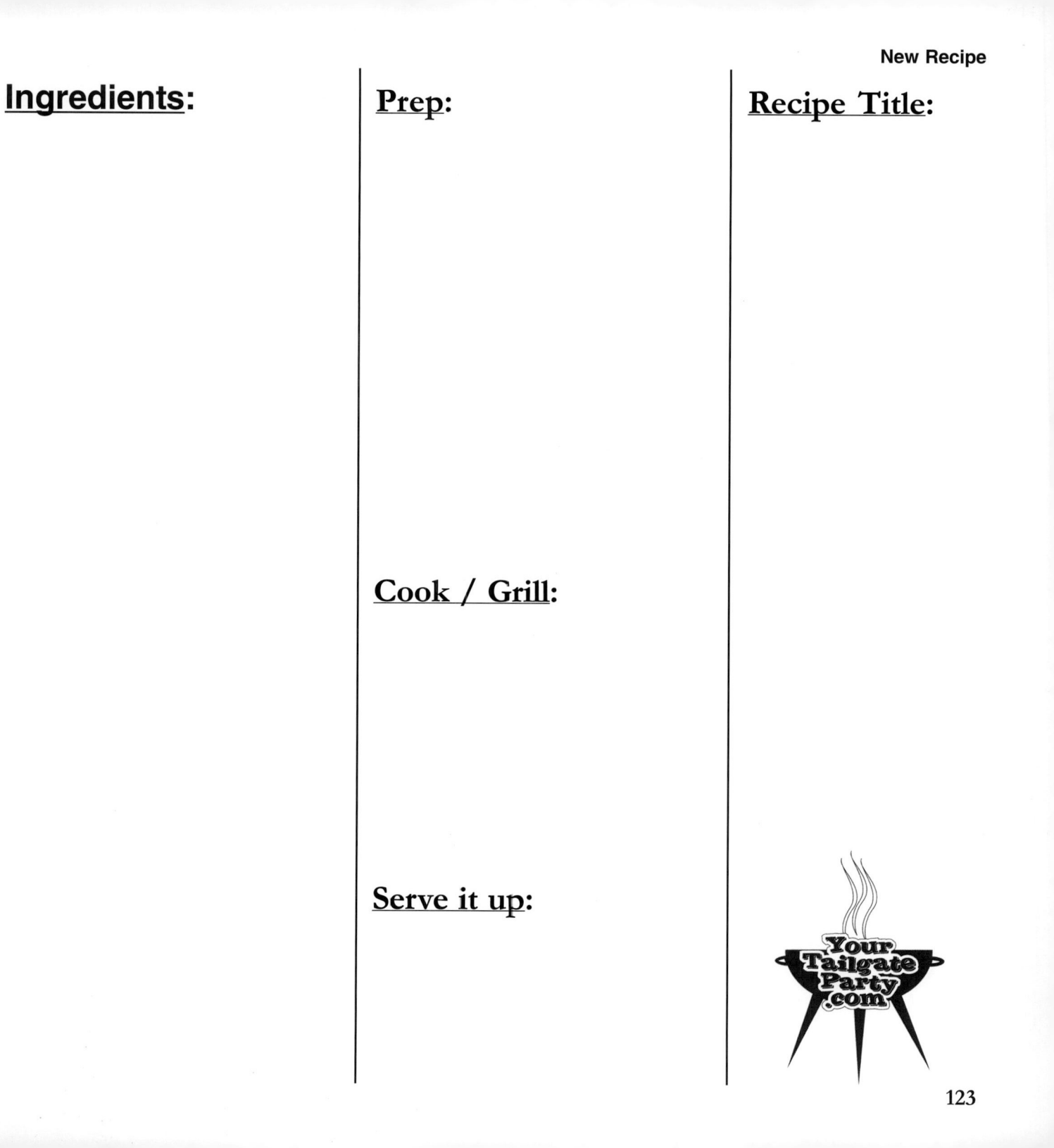

Recipe Title:

Ingredients:

Prep:

Cook / Grill:

Serve it up:

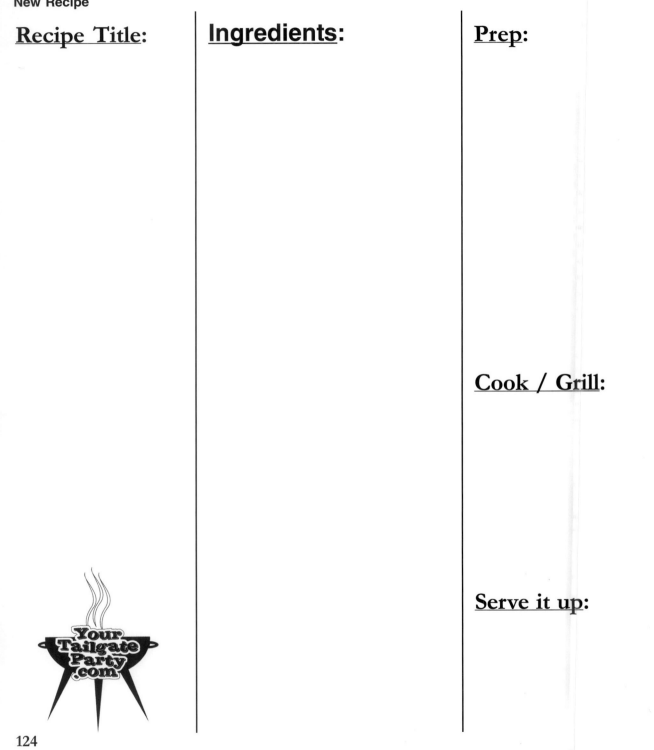

Ingredients:

Prep:

Cook / Grill:

Serve it up:

Recipe Title:

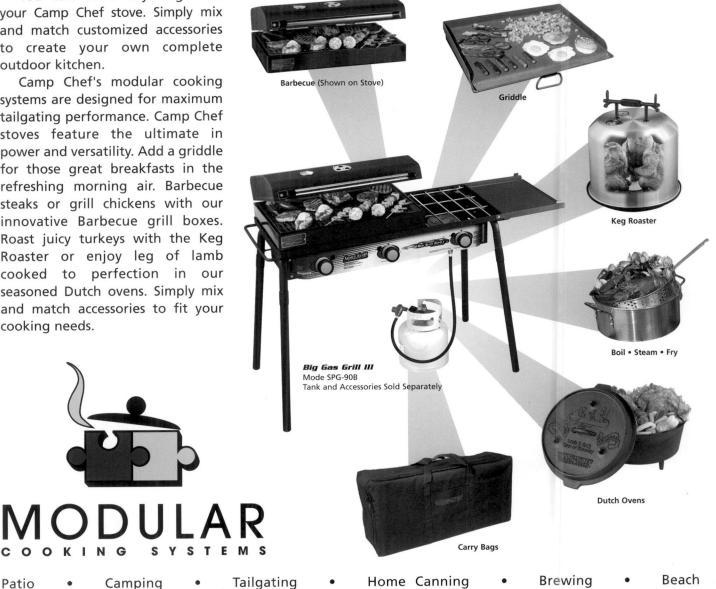